CONTEMPORARY EUROPEAN ARCHITECTS 2

CONTEMPORARY
EUROPEAN ARCHITECTS 2

BY DIRK MEYHÖFER

TASCHEN

KÖLN LISBOA LONDON NEW YORK OSAKA PARIS

Frontispiece · Frontispiz · Frontispice
Miralles y Pinós: Igualada Park and Cemetery, Barcelona (E)
© Photo: Hisao Suzuki

Page 6 · Seite 6 · Page 6
Gustav Peichl: Bundeskunsthalle, Bonn (D)
© Photo: Dieter Leistner

**This book was printed on 100 % chlorine-free bleached
paper in accordance with the TCF standard.**

© 1995 Benedikt Taschen GmbH
Hohenzollernring 53, D-50672 Köln

By Dirk Meyhöfer, Hamburg
Design: QART (Brodda, Hierholzer, Klaus), Hamburg
Cover design: Angelika Muthesius, Cologne; Mark Thomson, London
Text edited by Barbro Garenfeld Büning, Cologne
English translation: Christina Rathgeber, Berlin
French translation: Frédérique Daber, Lahors
German translation: Franca Fritz, Heinrich Koop, Cologne

Printed in Italy
ISBN 3-8228-9455-9

CONTENTS

HARMONIOUS PATCHWORK
EUROPEAN ARCHITECTURE IN THE 1990S

HARMONISCHES PATCHWORK
DIE EUROPÄISCHE ARCHITEKTUR DER 90ER JAHRE

UNE HARMONIE BIGARRÉE
L'ARCHITECTURE EUROPÉENNE DES ANNÉES 90

by Dirk **Meyhöfer** (Central Europa), Deyan **Sujic** (Western Europe)
and Clemens F. **Kusch** (Southern Europe)

European architecture in the early 1990s – on the threshold of the third millenium – is as vividly diverse as a patchwork quilt and yet, when taken together, still makes a harmonious impression. Europeans are proud of their continent's cultural diversity, of the different attitudes and dialects which can sometimes change within a very small geographic area, and it is this diversity which has given this continent its distinctive identity. As the problems to be found between Dublin and Istanbul or between Porto and St. Petersburg become ever more alike, and common laws and regulations within the European Community reinforce the effects of assimilation, the architectural styles of the different regions will also begin to resemble each other. But at present different styles still coexist.

And the details? By coincidence, two events – one in the fall of 1991 in Venice and the other in the summer of 1992 in Seville – have furnished clear insights into the performance standard of contemporary European architecture. The »Quinta Mostra Internazionale di Architettura 1991«, which took place in Venice, provided individual countries with the opportunity to present themselves in their own pavilions. The basic impression that had already been formed by the end of the 1980s was confirmed here: »modern architecture« – albeit revised and altered and without the technical and constructional susceptibilities of the 1920s and 1930s – has

Die europäische Architektur zu Beginn der 90er Jahre, also an der Schwelle zum dritten Jahrtausend, ist bunt zusammengewürfelt wie eine Patchworkdecke und ergibt trotzdem so etwas wie ein harmonisches Miteinander. Kulturelle Vielfalt: Das sind unterschiedliche Auffassungen und Dialekte, manchmal schon nach der Landkreisgrenze – das ist es, worauf der Erdteil stolz ist und was ihm seine unverwechselbare Identität gibt. Auch wenn die Probleme zwischen Dublin und Istanbul, zwischen Porto und St. Petersburg einander immer ähnlicher werden, wenn sich durch gemeinsames Recht und gleiche Vorschriften innerhalb der Europäischen Gemeinschaft die Assimilierungseffekte verstärken und sich damit auch die Architekturen der Regionen angleichen – noch existiert das Nebeneinander.

Und im einzelnen? Es fügte sich, daß zwei Ereignisse – eines im Herbst 1991 in Venedig, das andere im Sommer 1992 im andalusischen Sevilla – präzise Auskünfte über den Leistungsstandard der aktuellen europäischen Architektur gegeben haben. Die »Quinta Mostra Internazionale di Architettura 1991« hatte in Venedig den einzelnen Ländern die Gelegenheit gegeben, sich jeweils in ihrem Pavillon darzustellen. Es bestätigte sich dort der Eindruck, den wir schon zum Ende der 80er Jahre gewinnen mußten: Die »moderne Architektur«, inzwischen geläutert und gewandelt sowie technisch und konstruktiv nicht mehr so anfällig wie in den 20er und

Au début des années 90, au seuil du troisième millénaire, l'architecture européenne ressemble à un patchwork multicolore qui donnerait malgré tout une impression d'harmonie. La complexité culturelle: visions et langages divers, variant parfois d'une région à l'autre, voici ce que revendique cette partie du monde, voilà ce qui lui donne son inimitable originalité. Même si, de plus en plus, les problèmes sont les mêmes à Dublin et à Istanbul, à Porto et à Saint-Pétersbourg, même si une législation commune et des astreintes semblables renforcent l'effet d'assimilation et font apparaître un peu partout une architecture semblable, par bonheur, la coexistence des styles existe toujours.

Voyons la situation dans le détail. Deux événements – l'un en automne 1991 à Venise, l'autre en été 1992 à Séville – donnèrent une idée exacte du niveau de créativité de l'architecture européenne contemporaine. La «Quinta Mostra Internazionale di Architettura 1991», à Venise, offrit à chaque pays l'occasion de présenter son pavillon. L'impression générale, qui s'était fait jour dès la fin des années 80, se trouva confirmée: «l'architecture moderne», épurée, transformée, et dont les techniques de construction sont moins fragiles que dans les années 20 et les années 30, prend le pas sur l'architecture postmoderne. La petite prestation très réussie des Pays-Bas, intitulée «modernism without dogma», dans la lignée de De Stijl et du Bauhaus (et dont Hans Ibelings dit qu'elle

triumphed over Post-Modernism. It was impressive to see how the Netherlands, with its small but excellent presentation entitled, »Modernism without Dogma« followed in the footsteps of De Stijl and the Bauhaus and used »imagination and a wealth of forms« (Hans Ibelings) to repudiate the stylistic agitation of the host country's pavilion. In the pavilions belonging to what was at the time still the Soviet Union and Czechoslovakia, it was also apparent that when construction takes place on a larger scale in Eastern Europe, the link will be to the »status quo ante« of 1917 or 1930, that is to say, to Constructivism or Modernism. This will also mean that Modernism's position within architecture will be strengthened...

In the following summer, at the Seville Expo 1992, one could walk through the architectural exhibits. The presence of

30er Jahren, obsiegt über die Postmoderne. Beeindruckend, wie die Niederlande mit ihrer kleinen, feinen Präsentation »Modernism without dogma« auf den Spuren von De Stijl und Bauhaus auf »erfinderische und formenreiche Weise« (Hans Ibelings) die stilistischen Aufgeregtheiten im Gastgeberpavillon Italien sanft desavouierten.

Im damals sowjetischen Pavillon oder bei den Tschechoslowaken wurde ebenfalls deutlich: Wenn demnächst im Osten wieder in größerem Umfang gebaut werden sollte, dann wird man an den »Status quo ante« von 1917 oder 1930, also an Konstruktivismus oder Moderne, anknüpfen – und das bedeutet auch eine Stärkung der modernen Position innerhalb der Architektur...

Einen Sommer später, in Sevilla auf der Expo 1992, waren die Architekturexponate begehbar – über 100 Nationalpavillons machten die Expo zur »Weltausstellung der Architektur«. Europa zerfiel dabei noch einmal in zwei Blöcke: Die Oststaaten beschäftigten sich mit Vergangenheitsaufarbeitung. So baute die damalige ČSFR beispielsweise einen sehr funktionalistischen Container aus Holz (Architekten: Martin Némec, Jan Stempel) – eine Bauweise, wie sie zu sozialistischen Zeiten wenig willkommen war –, und Ungarns Stararchitekt Imre Makovecz stimmte mit seinem Pavillon einen sentimentalen Nachruf auf Ungarns Geschichte an. Die großen Industriestaaten aus Europas Westen blickten in die Zukunft und setzten, was

témoignait «d'un style inventif et d'une grande richesse formelle») apparut comme un désaveu face aux fantaisies stylistiques du pavillon des hôtes italiens. De la même façon, les pavillons ex-soviétique et tchécoslovaque firent la preuve que si, à l'Est, l'on doit se remettre à construire de façon conséquente ce sera à partir du status quo ante de 1917 ou de 1930, c'est-à-dire que l'on renouera avec le constructivisme ou le modernisme. Autant dire que, dans le monde de l'architecture, la position de l'architecture moderne s'en trouvera confortée...

L'été suivant, à l'Expo 92 de Séville, les réalisations étaient ouvertes au public: plus d'une centaine de pavillons représentant autant de pays firent de cet événement «l'exposition universelle de l'architecture». L'Europe s'y présentait en deux blocs est-ouest. Les États de l'Est avaient des comptes à régler avec leur passé. Ainsi, l'ancienne république socialiste de Tchécoslovaquie réalisa-t-elle un container de bois extrêmement fonctionnel (architectes: Martin Némec, Jan Stempel), procédé assez mal vu du temps du socialisme, et Imre Makovecz, la star de l'architecture hongroise, fit-il de son pavillon un chant dédié à l'histoire de son pays. Les grands Etats industriels de l'Europe de l'Ouest, tournés, eux, vers l'avenir, misèrent sur une architecture adaptée au climat (ce qui dans la chaleur brûlante de l'Andalousie était logique et même vital) et au niveau de conscience écologique grandissant.

more than 100 national pavilions made this World Exposition into an »international architectural exhibition«. Europe was once again divided into two blocs. The eastern European countries were still dealing with their past. For example, Czechoslovakia's extremely functionalist wooden container (architects: Martin Némec, Jan Stempel) represented a type of construction method which would not have been welcome during the Socialist era, and Hungary's star architect, Imre Makovecz, designed a pavilion which was a sentimental eulogy to Hungarian history. Western Europe's large industrial nations looked towards a future in which architecture responded sensibly towards the climate – a logical and even essential concern in view of the blazing Andalusian heat –

in der Gluthitze Andalusiens logisch, ja lebensnotwendig war, auf eine Architektur der Vernunft dem Klima und dem sich ändernden ökologischen Bewußtsein gegenüber. Ob Nicholas Grimshaws wassergekühlte Ausstellungsbox für Großbritannien oder Deutschlands Forum unter schattenbringendem Megapneu (Architekten: Mühlberger/Lippsmeier) – beide standen für eine Schwadron intelligenter Nationalpavillons, in denen sinnvoll Energie gespart wurde –, die Anforderungen an die Architektur der Zukunft ändern sich rasch.

Die Mitte: Deutschland

In Deutschland hatte es zum Ende der 80er Jahre zunächst keine Rezession gegeben. Im Gegenteil: Wiedervereini-

Tant la boîte-vitrine climatisée par circuit d'eau de Nicholas Grimshaw, pour la Grande-Bretagne, que le forum allemand ombragé par un méga-pneu (architectes: Mühlberger/Lippsmeier) témoignaient d'une tendance bien adaptée à l'économie d'énergie: les besoins de l'architecture des temps à venir sont en constante évolution.

Le centre: l'Allemagne

A la fin des années 80 la récession n'était nullement perceptible en Allemagne. Au contraire: la réunification et la rumeur qui faisait de Berlin la nouvelle capitale suscitèrent des impulsions, attirèrent des architectes du monde entier qui, chez eux, n'avaient guère l'occasion de réaliser leurs projets. L'Allemagne est alors aussi pleine d'architectes

and also reflected a changing ecological consciousness. Both Nicholas Grimshaw's water-cooled exhibition box for Great Britain and Germany's forum under shady mega-pneu (architects: Mühlberger/Lippsmeier) – can be taken as representative of an entire squadron of intelligent national pavilions concerned with the conservation of energy. The requirements for the architecture of the future can change quickly.

The Middle: Germany

In Germany there was no sign of a recession in the late 1980s. On the contrary, reunification and the flurry of activities surrounding Berlin's regained status as the capital, provided new impulses and attracted foreign architects who were no longer able to realize projects in their own countries. In a manner of speaking, Germany offers the attrac-

gung und der Rummel um die neue Hauptstadt Berlin setzten Impulse, lockten Architekten aus aller Welt an, die kaum noch Projekte im eigenen Lande verwirklichen können. Deutschland ist von ausländischen Architekturstars so überlaufen wie ein Kaufhaus beim Sommerschlußverkauf. Alle sind sie da: Peter Eisenman, Zaha Hadid, Richard Meier, Jean Nouvel, Arata Isozaki, Shin Takamatsu und viele mehr.

Außerdem hat eine Art Wachablösung stattgefunden: Die Garde der großen deutschen Nachkriegsarchitekten tritt ab. Die Rationalisten Josef Paul Kleihues und Oswald Mathias Ungers oder der Expressionist Gottfried Böhm haben bis in die späten 80er Jahre für weltweite Resonanz gesorgt. Nun lassen sie über hohen Auftragsbestand Innovationskraft missen. Allein Günter Behnisch setzt für sich und Deutschland mit dem Spätwerk noch einmal Akzente: Sein neuer Bonner Bundestag wird der Demokratie als Bauherr auf sensible Weise gerecht: eine gläserne Inkunabel in den Rheinwiesen.

Eine weitere Architektengeneration in Deutschland ist nachgewachsen: Mitt- und Endvierziger, die sehr unterschiedlich, sehr individuell und sehr engagiert arbeiten – meist in Gruppen zusammengefaßt wie das Darmstädter Konstruktivisten-Duo Eisele & Fritz oder das Postmodernentrio Berghof, Landes, Rang oder deren Geistesverwandte Jourdan und Müller (alle aus Frankfurt/Main). Aber es gibt auch noch Einzelkämpfer

étrangers qu'un grand magasin de clients, un jour de soldes. Ils sont tous là: Peter Eisenman, Zaha Hadid, Richard Meier, Jean Nouvel, Arata Isozaki, Shin Takamatsu, pour ne citer qu'eux.

De plus, une sorte de relève s'est faite: la garde des grands architectes allemands de l'après-guerre se retire. Les rationalistes Josef Paul Kleihues et Oswald Mathias Ungers ou l'expressionniste Gottfried Böhm ont porté la réputation de l'architecture allemande dans le monde entier. Mais trop de commandes finissent par nuire à leur inventivité. Seule l'œuvre de vieillesse de Günter Behnisch reste marquante. A Bonn, son nouveau Parlement témoigne du système démocratique qui l'a fait ériger: c'est un incunable de verre transparent posé sur les prairies, au bord du Rhin. A présent, une nouvelle génération d'architectes est apparue: ils sont au milieu ou à la fin de leur quarantaine et ils travaillent de façon très diverse, très originale et très engagée. Ils se sont souvent constitués en groupes, tel le duo des constructivistes Eisele & Fritz, de Darmstadt ou le trio postmoderne Berghof, Landes, Rang ou encore, spirituellement proches, Jourdan et Müller (tous de Francfort/Main).

Mais il y aussi des solitaires comme Hans Kollhoff ou Axel Schultes, de Berlin, Stefan Braunfels, de Munich et Christoph Mäckler, de Francfort dont le point commun est de faire partie de l'avant-garde allemande, si toutefois on peut encore employer cette expression.

Architecture from Germany II – with a new self-confidence. Left: Kunstmuseum Bonn (Axel Schultes). Below: Deutsche Bank in Luxembourg (Gottfried Böhm)

Architektur aus Deutschland II – mit neuem Selbstbewußtsein. Links: Kunstmuseum Bonn (Axel Schultes). Unten: Deutsche Bank in Luxemburg (Gottfried Böhm)

Architecture made in Germany II – forte d'une nouvelle confiance en soi. A gauche: Kunstmuseum à Bonn (Axel Schultes). En bas: Deutsche Bank à Luxembourg (Gottfried Böhm)

tions of a department store during an end-of-season sale. Distinguished architects from all over the world can be found there: Peter Eisenman, Zaha Hadid, Richard Meier, Jean Nouvel, Arata Isozaki, Shin Takamatsu and many others.

Moreover, there has been a changing of the guard in Germany. The old guard of post-war architects is leaving the field. The Rationalists, Josef Paul Kleihues and Oswald Mathias Ungers and the Expressionist, Gottfried Böhm, enjoyed international acclaim right up to the end of the 1980s. Because they now have many commissions, their current work lacks innovative energy. Amongst this generation only Günter Behnisch has once again struck a new note for himself and for Germany with his late work. His recent parliamentary building in Bonn – a transparent glass incunabulum beside the Rhine – gives full and sensitive expression to the claims of the democratic process.

A new generation of German architects has emerged. In their mid-to-late forties, they work in very different, individual and committed ways. They are generally to be found in groups, such as the Darmstadt Constructivist duo, Eisele & Fritz, the Post-Modern trio, Berghof, Landes, Rang or their kindred spirits, Jourdan and Müller. All of these groups are based in Frankfurt/Main.

There are, however, still prominent architects who work on their own, such as Hans Kollhoff and Axel Schultes in

wie Hans Kollhoff oder Axel Schultes aus Berlin, Stefan Braunfels aus München und Christoph Mäckler aus Frankfurt. Ihnen ist gemein, daß sie als Deutschlands Avantgarde gelten könnten, wenn ein solcher Begriff überhaupt noch zulässig ist. Alle vier machen eine Architektur, die wieder mehr durch Form denn Ornament gekennzeichnet ist. Allen ist gemeinsam, daß Rebellion auf ihrem Panier steht: Protest gegen das gewohnte Gleichmaß. Ungers-Schüler Kollhoff schlägt für Berlin Hochhäuser als Antwort auf das bekannte Traufenhöhendiktat vor. Stefan Braunfels, der das Münchner Museum für moderne Kunst bauen will, begehrt gegen die manierierte Großmannsbausucht des bayrischen Freistaats auf.

Um noch mehr Einsicht in die deutsche Architektur zu erlangen, lohnt auch die regionale Betrachtung im föderalistischen Deutschland. In »boom-town« Hamburg hat man sich dabei am weitesten vorgewagt, was eine Definition des eigenen Stils betrifft: mit dem heimischen Backstein, den man in schönen Gegensatz zu Glas und Stahl setzen kann, knüpft man an die große Zeit der Kontorhäuser aus den 20er Jahren (z. B. Chilehaus) und eigene Traditionen an. Eine davon betrifft das Schiffsmotiv, das ausgerechnet zwei Münchner, die Architekten Uwe Kiessler und Otto Steidle, für den Neubau des Verlages Gruner und Jahr bemüht haben. Direkt an der Elbe gelegen, grüßt nun eine Art »Verlagswerft« mit Zinkblechfassaden und

Tous les quatre produisent des œuvres dans lesquelles les volumes prennent le pas sur les éléments décoratifs. Tous brandissent la bannière de la rébellion et refusent l'uniformisation devenue règle. La règle veut qu'on ne construise pas au-dessus d'une certaine hauteur? Kollhoff, élève de Ungers, propose d'ériger des tours à Berlin. Stefan Braunfels, qui sera l'architecte du Musée d'art moderne de Munich, s'insurge contre la folie des grandeurs qui règne dans l'Etat libre de Bavière. Pour une vision plus précise de l'architecture en Allemagne, pays à l'organisation fédérale, l'approche régionale peut être intéressante. En matière de style, c'est à Hambourg, ville du boom économique, qu'on est allé le plus loin. Avec la brique locale, qui for-

Berlin, Stefan Braunfels in Munich and Christoph Mäckler in Frankfurt. They could be considered as part of Germany's avant-garde – if such a term can even be used anymore. All four of them create architecture which is once again characterized more by form than by ornament. All of them have taken a rebellious stance in protesting against prescribed architectural uniformity. Kollhoff, a disciple of Ungers, has responded to Berlin's notorious height restrictions by proposing highrises for the inner city. Stefan Braunfels, who will be the architect of the Museum for Modern Art in Munich, has rejected the mannered, status-conscious style of building prevalent in Bavaria.

One can gain a more ordered picture of German architecture if one also considers its regional manifestations in this federalist state. The boom-town of Hamburg has ventured furthest in the attempt at defining an individual style. The revival in the use of local brick not only provides a handsome contrast to glass and steel, but also recalls the great office buildings built during the 1920s (e. g. Chilehaus) and is closely linked to local traditions. One of these traditions is the ship motif, and it is somehow ironic that it has been two architects from Munich, Uwe Kiessler and Otto Steidle, who have used this motif for their new building for the Gruner und Jahr publishing house. One is now greeted by a sort of »publishing shipyard« on the banks of the Elbe. With its

schräggestellten Stützen und versucht mit der Bildwelt des benachbarten Hafens zu konkurrieren. Wenige Kilometer entfernt, an der Alster, hat Jochem Jourdan das Verlagsgebäude von Hoffmann und Campe in die Villenpracht Harvestehudes gesetzt. Dort ist ein Verlagsschlößchen entstanden mit einem Tempelchen auf dem Dach und vergoldeten Geländern in der Treppenhalle. Beide Häuser sind in ihrer Unterschiedlichkeit in einem Punkt ähnlich: Sie sprechen jeweils das (Architektur-)Idiom ihrer unmittelbaren Umgebung, pflegen den Regionalismus.

Berlin wird hingegen wie zu Zeiten der Internationalen Bauausstellung (IBA) in den 80er Jahren jetzt erst recht ein internationaler Ort sein mit einem Potsdamer Platz à la Renzo Piano und Helmut Jahn, einem Reichstag von Norman Foster oder Santiago Calatrava. Figuren

me un beau contraste avec le verre et l'acier, on a renoué avec la grande époque des comptoirs des années 20 (la Maison du Chili) et les traditions locales, le thème du bateau, par exemple. Deux Munichois, Uwe Kiessler et Otto Steidle, ont choisi de l'illustrer par le nouveau bâtiment de la maison d'édition Gruner und Jahr. Située en bordure de l'Elbe, une sorte de «quai de l'édition» avec ses façades recouvertes de feuilles d'étain et ses contreforts obliques tente de rivaliser avec le port voisin. A quelques kilomètres de là, au bord de l'Alster, Jochem Jourdan a installé la maison d'édition de Hoffmann und Campe dans le quartier des luxueuses villas de Harvestehude. Il en a fait un castelet dont le toit comporte un petit temple et l'escalier d'entrée des balustrades dorées. Les deux édifices, avec toutes leurs différences, ont un point commun:

Pictorial architecture. Publishing shipyard
for Gruner und Jahr in Hamburg (Kiessler
und Steidle).

Bildhaftes Bauen. Verlagswerft für Gruner
und Jahr in Hamburg (Kiessler und Steidle).

Architecture pittoresque. «Quai de l'édition» pour Gruner und Jahr à Hambourg
(Kiessler et Steidle).

sheet-zinc façades and oblique supports, the building attempts to compete with the colourful world of the neighbouring harbour. Jochem Jourdan's building for another publishing house – Hoffmann und Campe – can be found only a few kilometres away, beside the Alster, in the midst of the magnificent mansions of Harvestehude. A small publishing palace has been created here. Its roof is adorned by a miniature temple and gilded banisters decorate its stairwell. Despite all of their differences, the two buildings are similar in one respect: they each lend expression to the (architectural) idiom of their immediate environment, thereby fostering regionalism.

In contrast, Berlin – with a Potsdamer Platz à la Renzo Piano and a Reichstag by either Norman Foster or Santiago Calatrava – will develop into even more of an international site than it was during the period of the International Building Exposition (IBA) in the 1980s. The unconventional and cosmopolitan Daniel Libeskind will remain in Berlin at least until his »lightning flash«, the new Jewish Museum, is completed. Without such innovative personalities the investors would go elsewhere.

Frankfurt's skyline is assaulted by second-rate highrises in »lipstick design« (convention tower, Helmut Jahn) or a faceless radical structure with a hat brim (DG-Bank, Kohn, Peddersen, Fox). Apart from such constructions, there is only the past glory of the Museumsufer, a

wie der Querdenker und Kosmopolit Daniel Libeskind, der zumindest so lange in Berlin bleibt, bis sein steinerner »Blitz«, das neue jüdische Museum, vollendet ist, sind das Salz in einer Suppe, in die sonst die Investoren spucken.

Frankfurt läßt den Himmel mit zweitklassigen Wolkenkratzern im »Lippenstiftdesign« (Messeturm, Helmut Jahn) oder gesichtslosen Rundlingen mit Hutkrempe (DG-Bank, Kohn, Peddersen, Fox) stürmen. Ansonsten lebt die Mainmetropole vom verflossenen Ruhm ihres Museumsufers, dessen explosionsartige Karriere zum Boulevard der Architektur (Ungers, Meier, Peichl u. a.) nach einem Machtwechsel im Kulturdezernat verpufft ist.

Und dann gibt es noch Bonn, das sich als Hauptstadt architektonisch manifestieren wollte: Neben dem Bundestag sind 1992 zwei weitere Großbauten fertiggestellt worden: Bundeskunsthalle und Kunstmuseum Bonn. Axel Schultes stellt sein Kunstmuseum hinter eine hohe Wand, die nicht nur Schutz gegen die laute Godesberger Allee liefert, sondern auch Voraussetzungen für eine steinerne Achse für Bonn schafft. Eine neue, in Nachkriegsdeutschland bisher unbekannte Monumentalität entsteht, und Axel Schultes wird dies in Berlin mit seinen Entwürfen für das Regierungsviertel im Spreebogen fortsetzen wollen. Gustav Peichls Bonner Bundeskunsthalle strotzt ebenfalls vor Selbstbewußtsein: »Sechzehn nackte, rostbraune Cortenstahl-Säulen – sie symbolisieren

ils s'expriment dans l'idiome (architectural) de leur environnement et pratiquent le régionalisme.

Berlin, par contre, devient, comme au temps de l'exposition d'architecture internationale (IBA) des années 80, un lieu de plus en plus cosmopolite avec sa place de Potsdam vue par Renzo Piano et Helmut Jahn, son Reichstag par Norman Foster ou Santiago Calatrava. Des gens comme Daniel Libeskind, ce citoyen du monde peu conventionnee qui restera berlinois du moins le temps que s'achève le nouveau musée juif, sont le sel d'une soupe dans laquelle, si ce n'était pour ces hommes, les investisseurs cracheraient.

A Francfort s'élèvent des tours de moindre intérêt, en «bâtons de rouge à lèvres» (tour des expositions, par Helmut Jahn) ou des rotondités sans visage dotées d'un rebord de chapeau (banque DG, de Kohn, Peddersen, Fox). A côté de cela, la ville vit de la gloire passée du quartier des musées, ancienne vitrine de l'architecture (Ungers, Meier, Peichl, entre autres), qui s'est éteinte après un changement de pouvoir au sein du Ministère de la culture.

Et puis il y a Bonn qui, en tant que capitale, entendait bien faire parler de son architecture. En 1992, en plus du Parlement, deux grands projets ont été réalisés: la Bundeskunsthalle et le Musée d'art de la ville de Bonn. Axel Schultes place ce dernier derrière un haut mur qui n'est pas seulement une protection contre le bruit de la Godesberger Allee

collection of museums along the banks of the Main. Its dynamic development as an architectural boulevard (Ungers, Meier, Peichl and others) has now fallen flat as a result of political changes in the city's cultural administration.

And then there is still Bonn, which wanted architectural manifestations of its status as the capital city. Apart from the Bundestag, two other major buildings were completed here in 1992: the Bundeskunsthalle (Federal Art Exhibition Hall) and the Kunstmuseum Bonn (Bonn Museum of Art). Axel Schultes placed the Kunstmuseum behind a high wall, and thereby not only provided protection against the loud traffic on Godesberger Allee but also created the prerequisites for a stone axis for the city. With this museum, a monumentality was created which had hitherto been unknown in post-war Germany, and Axel Schultes will want to continue in this vein with his designs for the Spreebogen in Berlin. Gustav Peichl's Bundeskunsthalle in Bonn bristles with a similar type of self-confidence: »Sixteen bare, rust-brown, Corten steel columns – symbolizing the sixteen states of the Federal Republic – flank the street front, and the building thereby makes a grand entrance into the urban landscape« (Gottfried Knapp).

How can Germany's architectural scene at the beginning of the 1990s best be summarized? It is complex, international and regional, old and young, but also more introverted than extroverted.

die sechzehn Bundesländer – flankieren die Front zur Straße hin, machen aus dem Auftritt des Bauwerks in der Stadtlandschaft einen pompösen Kondukt« (Gottfried Knapp).

Deutschlands Architekturszene zu Beginn der 90er Jahre? Vielschichtig: international und regional; alt und jung, allerdings eher introvertiert als extrovertiert.

Österreich und Nordschweiz

Gustav Peichl schlägt die Brücke zur österreichischen und Wiener Architektur, die immer noch zwei unterschiedliche Welten bedeuten: ein ehrlicher Regionalismus aus Holz, Putz und Bescheidenheit für das Land zwischen Vorarlberg und Neusiedler See, dagegen die metropolitane Mischung aus Glimmer, Spinnerei und Avantgarde in Wien selbst – für Läden, Restaurants oder Bars.

mais qui jette les bases d'un axe de pierre pour la ville. Le résultat a quelque chose de monumental, tel qu'on ne l'avait jamais vu dans l'Allemagne d'après guerre, et que Schultes paraît vouloir poursuivre dans ses projets pour le quartier administratif de Spreebogen, à Berlin. La Bundeskunsthalle de Gustav Peichl ne manque pas non plus de prétention: «Seize colonnes d'acier (Corten), nues, brun-rouille, symbolisant les seize länder fédéraux, bordent l'espace qui sépare l'édifice de la rue et lui donnent, dans le paysage urbain, un aspect pompeux» (Gottfried Knapp).

Que peut-on dire de la scène architecturale allemande au début des années 90? Qu'elle est complexe, tout à la fois internationale et régionaliste, vieille et jeune mais sûrement plus introvertie qu'extravertie.

Austria and Northern Switzerland

Gustav Peichl is forging a symbolic link between Austrian and Viennese architecture. They still represent two different worlds. The one is an honest regionalism, constructed of wood, plaster and unassuming attitudes for the area between Vorarlberg and Neusiedlersee, the country in general. In contrast to this is Vienna's urban mixture of glitter, craziness and avant-garde, meant for stores, restaurants and bars.

The real achievement in Austria still remains – or has once more become – its

Die eigentliche Leistung indes ist immer noch oder wieder der österreichische Wohnungsbau, der inzwischen auch fleißig nach Deutschland exportiert wird (z. B. Berlin Britz-Süd, München-Puchheim). Es ist die gute Wohnungsbautradition zwischen den Weltkriegen, die als Grund angeführt werden könnte, vielleicht auch das, was der Architekt Adolf Krischanitz so umschreibt: »In Österreich ist eine Wohnung immer noch ein soziales Gut und nicht nur Ware!« Und dieses soziale Gut kommt in unterschiedlichen Kleidern auf den Markt.

L'Autriche et le nord de la Suisse

C'est Gustav Peichl qui jette un pont symbolique entre l'architecture autrichienne et celle proprement viennoise qui représentent aujourd'hui encore deux mondes distincts: un franc régionalisme fait de bois, de crépi et de modestie pour le territoire compris entre les monts du Vorarlberg et le Neusiedlersee. Et puis, face à cela, dans la métropole, le mélange de brillant, de folle fantaisie et d'avant-garde qui s'exprime dans ses magasins, ses restaurants, ses bars. Toutefois, le véritable exploit

housing construction. This has often been exported to Germany (e. g. Berlin Britz-Süd, Munich-Puchheim). The Austrians can draw on a solid tradition of inter-war housing construction, but there could also be another reason for its high quality. The architect Adolf Krischanitz has described this reason in the following way: »In Austria an apartment still has social value and is not merely a product!« This social value is expressed in different ways. It can be urban and detached, like the castellated construction on Traviatagasse (Carl Pruscha and others). It can be found behind a gigantic, noise-reducing glass curtain as on Brunnerstrasse (Helmut Richter). It can also appear in an idyllic setting of terraced houses, whose ingenious ground plans are modelled on designs by Adolf Loos, as in the suburb of Aspern (Adolf Krischanitz). And of course the good examples are not restricted to the boundaries of Vienna and the vicinities. A visit to »Graz Pragmatism« (Orhan Kipcak) and to other Austrian towns can be recommended.

The inevitable changing of the guard has also taken place in Austria. Noteworthy architects are not just the »big three« of Hans Hollein, Wilhelm Holzbauer and Gustav Peichl and the rebellious boys who call themselves COOP Himmelblau, but also such figures as Adolf Krischanitz, Elsa Prochazka, Lainer/Auer, Hermann Czech and Günther Domenig. All of them act, i. e., they design in a way that »looks to the future and is incon-

Städtisch und abgeschottet wie eine Burg in der Traviatagasse (Carl Pruscha u. a.), hinter einem gigantischen, lärmabweisenden Glasvorhang in der Brunnerstraße (Helmut Richter) oder als Reihenhausidylle mit ausgeklügelten Grundrissen nach Vorbildern eines Adolf Loos in der Vorstadt Aspern (Adolf Krischanitz). Und natürlich beschränken sich die guten Beispiele nicht auf Wien – eine Reise zum »Grazer Pragmatismus« (Orhan Kipcak) und anderswohin wird empfohlen.

Auch in Österreich hat die unvermeidliche Wachablösung stattgefunden. Zu den großen Drei – Hans Hollein, Wilhelm Holzbauer und Gustav Peichl – und den aufmüpfigen Boys von COOP Himmelblau treten Adolf Krischanitz, Elsa Prochazka oder Lainer/Auer, Hermann Czech oder Günther Domenig. Sie alle entwerfen in einer Art, die »in die Zukunft schaut und ohne Vergangenheit nicht denkbar ist« (Hans Hollein).

In Wien-Aspern – auch das kann als weiterer Nachweis einer engen Verquikkung in Mitteleuropa gewertet werden – bauten auch die Basler Architekten Jacques Herzog und Pierre de Meuron vorbildliche Reihenhäuser. Beide sind Vertreter einer neuen Schweizer und damit europäischen Architektur, die sich sehr stark mit differenzierter Wahrnehmung auseinandersetzt und deren Fassaden entsprechend diffizil zu betrachten sind. Die anderen Helden der Schweizer Szene wie Magazzini, Ricola und Laufer, Diener und Diener, Theo

de cette architecture concerne toujours, ou bien à nouveau, la construction de logements qui, depuis un certain temps, s'exporte gaillardement en Allemagne (par exemple à Berlin Britz-Süd ou à Munich-Puchheim).

On pourrait expliquer le phénomène par le fait de cette bonne vieille tradition de l'habitat de l'entre-deux guerres ou par ce que décrit l'architecte Adolf Krischanitz en ces termes: «En Autriche, un logement reste un bien social, il n'est pas devenu simple marchandise!» Et ce bien social se présente sous divers atours. Urbain et clos comme un château fort dans la Traviatagasse (Carl Pruscha, entre autres), protégé par un gigantesque mur de verre anti-bruit dans la Brunnerstrasse (Helmut Richter) ou en rangée idyllique de petits pavillons aux plans très raffinés, inspirés d'un Adolf Loos, à Aspern, dans la banlieue de Vienne (Adolf Krischanitz). Mais bien sûr les exemples positifs ne se trouvent pas uniquement dans la commune de Vienne, un voyage au centre du «pragmatisme de Graz» (Orhan Kipcak) s'impose.

En Autriche aussi, l'inévitable relève de la garde a eu lieu. Aux Trois Grands – Hans Hollein, Wilhelm Holzbauer et Gustav Peichl – et aux rebelles de la COOP Himmelblau se joignent Adolf Krischanitz, Elsa Prochazka ou Lainer/Auer, Hermann Czech ou Günther Domenig. Tous travaillent selon une méthode qui «tournée vers l'avenir est impensable sans le passé.» (Hans Hollein)

Austrian architecture is still famous for its exemplary housing, which is also exported, for example, to Germany. Social housing in Berlin-Britz (Fritz Matzinger)

Die österreichische Architektur ist nach wie vor bekannt für ihren vorbildlichen Wohnungsbau und wird exportiert – beispielsweise auch – nach Deutschland: Sozialwohnungen in Berlin-Britz (Fritz Matzinger)

L'architecture autrichienne est connue pour sa construction locative, qui s'exporte, entre autres, en Allemagne: logements sociaux à Berlin-Britz (Fritz Matzinger)

ceivable without the past« (Hans Hollein).

In the Viennese suburb of Aspern two architects from Basle – Jacques Herzog and Pierre De Meuron – built exemplary terraced houses. This too can be taken as further proof of the close intermingling that is currently occurring in Central Europe.

They can be understood as representatives of a new Swiss and thereby of a new European architecture. It is a form of architecture intensely concerned with differentiated perceptions, and accordingly, its façades often pose difficulties for the observer. Common to the other heroes of the Swiss scene – Magazzini, Ricola and Laufer, Diener and Diener, Theo Hotz as well as Peter Zumthor – is their adherence to a very austere unassuming modernity.

Hotz sowie Peter Zumthor haben alle gemein, daß sie eine sehr arme, bescheidene Modernität an den Tag legen. Dies hat in der Schweizer Architektur des 20. Jahrhunderts schon Tradition.

Der Westen: Großbritannien

Nick Grimshaws neue Bahnhofshalle für die Londoner Waterloo Station gilt als das bedeutendste Bauwerk, das 1994 in Großbritannien fertiggestellt wird. »Waterloo« ist die nördliche Endstation für Züge, die durch den Kanaltunnel von Paris und Brüssel nach London und zurück fahren.

Dieser Bahnhof ist nicht nur aus gestalterischer Sicht bedeutend, sondern in erster Linie als eine Art Wendepunkt in der britischen Architekturentwicklung. Zunächst einmal handelt es sich um ein aufsehenerregendes Bauwerk, einen

A Vienne-Aspern – et c'est un exemple qui permet de rejeter l'idée que l'Europe centrale se replie sur elle-même – les architectes bâlois Jacques Herzog et Pierre de Meuron ont construit des petites maisons exemplaires. Ils représentent une nouvelle architecture suisse, et donc européenne, qui se prononce pour une conception différenciée de la construction et dont les réalisations sont, en conséquence, d'un abord difficile. Les autres héros du milieu suisse comme Magazzini, Ricola et Laufer, Diener und Diener, Theo Hotz et aussi Peter Zumthor ont tous en commun un modernisme aride et modeste qui a ses racines dans la tradition architecturale suisse du 20ème siècle.

L'Ouest: La Grande-Bretagne

Le hall de la gare de Waterloo, par Nick Grimshaw, à Londres, passe pour être le bâtiment le plus important de l'année 1994 en Grande-Bretagne. La gare de Waterloo est le terminus nord des trains qui empruntent le tunnel sous la Manche de Paris et Bruxelles à Londres.

L'édifice n'est pas seulement signifiant dans sa conception. Il représente avant tout une sorte de tournant dans l'évolution de l'architecture britannique. Il s'agit tout d'abord d'une construction impressionnante, digne héritière des grandes gares victoriennes, pourvu d'une toiture remarquable d'acier et de verre. L'importance de la gare de Waterloo ne réside pas seulement dans ce qui est mais aussi dans ce qui n'est pas. Il

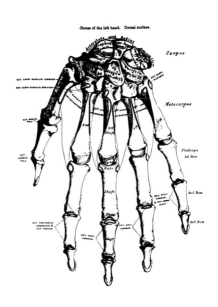

This has always been a tradition of Swiss architecture of the 20th century.

The West: Great Britain

Nick Grimshaw's new concourse for Waterloo Station in London is considered to be the most important building of 1994 in Great Britain. »Waterloo« is the northern terminus for trains travelling through the Channel tunnel from Paris and Brussels to London.

This train station is important not only in terms of its design, but above all because it represents something akin to a turning-point in architectural development in Great Britain. With its masterly roof structure of steel and glass, the building itself is a sensational construction and a worthy successor to the great Victorian train stations. The significance of Waterloo Station, however, lies not

würdigen Nachfolger der großen viktorianischen Bahnhöfe – mit einer meisterhaften Dachkonstruktion aus Stahl und Glas. Die Bedeutung von Waterloo Station liegt nicht nur in dem, was ist, sondern auch in dem, was nicht ist. Denn es handelt sich um kein Bürogebäude, kein Einkaufszentrum und kein Spekulationsobjekt von der Stange, das den Bedürfnissen des Durchschnitts folgen müßte. Der neue Schnellbahnhof ist vielmehr eines der wenigen Beispiele maßgeschneiderter Architektur, das im Auftrag der britischen Öffentlichkeit gebaut wurde.

Zur Zeit des Baubooms der 80er Jahre war London ein internationales Bauparadies, das amerikanische Architekten anlockte und Investitionsgelder von Tokio bis Oslo (und aller dazwischenliegenden Orte) fließen ließ; aber diese private

ne s'agit pas en effet d'un immeuble de bureaux, ni d'un centre commercial ni d'un quelconque objet de spéculation destiné à satisfaire les besoins d'une clientèle ordinaire. Cette nouvelle gare est bel et bien un des rares exemples d'une construction sur mesure résultant d'une commande de l'Etat anglais.

A l'époque du boom des années 80, Londres était le paradis international des constructeurs et attirait des architectes américains et des investisseurs de Tokyo à Oslo. Mais cette abondance de commandes privées eut pour conséquence l'appauvrissement du patrimoine public. Tandis que la silhouette de la ville ressemblait de plus en plus à une forêt de tours bardées de marbre et de cours intérieures strictement gardées, les voies de transport nationales et municipales étaient laissées à l'abandon et

Swan-song of the commercial architecture
of the Thatcher era: Ralph Erskine's The
Ark – a new type of office building with ecological ambitions in the London Borough of
Hammersmith

Schwanengesang auf die kommerzielle Architektur der Thatcher-Ära: Ralph Erskines
The Ark – ein neuer Typus des Bürohauses
mit ökologischen Ambitionen in London-
Hammersmith

Chant du cygne pour l'architecture commerciale de l'ère Thatcher: l'«Arche» de Ralph
Erskine – une nouvelle conception, aux ambitions écologiques, de la construction de
bureaux à Londres-Hammersmith

only in that which it is, but also in that which it is not. It is neither an office building nor a shopping centre, nor is it a speculator's project that had to be tailored to the needs of the average customer. Instead, this new, rapid-transit train station is one of the few examples of made-to-measure architecture publicly commissioned in Britain.

During the building boom of the 1980s, London was an international builder's paradise. It attracted American architects and investors from Tokyo to Oslo – and all points in between. The indirect result of this proliferation in the private building sector, however, was the neglect of public assets. While London's skyline was being transformed into a forest of marble-clad office towers with carefully guarded atriums, the national and municipal traffic system was allowed to deteriorate and the construction of social housing came to a complete standstill.

The boom provided large-scale opportunities to a generation of relatively young architects. Men and women in their thirties, who would otherwise have been working in large firms with the aim of eventually opening their own offices, now had the chance to do exactly that. This gold-rush atmosphere led to the construction of an entire series of extravagant new office towers and elegant restaurants and stores. The change came in 1988. Following the stock-market crash, a bleaker reality set in. What was significant here was not only the

. Pracht führte indirekt zur Verwahrlosung des öffentlichen Besitzes. Während sich Londons Skyline in einen Wald von marmorverkleideten Bürotürmen mit sorgfältig bewachten Atrien verwandelte, wurde das staatliche und kommunale Verkehrssystem seinem Verfall überlassen, und der soziale Wohnungsbau kam zum völligen Stillstand.

Der Boom bot einer Generation von relativ jungen Architekten die Möglichkeit, im großen Stil zu bauen. Männer und Frauen, die sonst während ihres dritten Lebensjahrzehnts als Assistenten und Assistentinnen großer Firmen darauf hingearbeitet hätten, sich selbständig zu machen, konnten das jetzt schon tun. In dieser Goldgräberstimmung entstand eine ganze Reihe extravaganter neuer Bürotürme, eleganter Restaurants und Geschäfte – bis zum Börsenkrach des Jahres 1988. Er trübte das Bild und

la construction de logements sociaux en arriva au point mort.

Le boom offrait à une génération d'architectes relativement jeunes une occasion de s'illustrer. Des hommes et des femmes dans leur trentaine qui auraient normalement occupé des postes d'assistants dans de grosses entreprises avec l'idée de se mettre un jour à leur compte purent le faire sans plus attendre. Dans cette ambiance de ruée vers l'or s'élevèrent d'extravagants immeubles professionnels, d'élégants restaurants et magasins – jusqu'à l'effondrement de la bourse en 1988. En conséquence, non seulement beaucoup de bâtiments ne furent jamais loués, leurs promoteurs, et certains architectes, firent faillite mais toute l'école postmoderne britannique, intimement liée à ce boom, en pâtit.

Nicholas Grimshaw fut un des seuls architectes de sa génération à ne pas participer à la construction de tous ces bureaux. Ce n'est que récemment qu'il réalise de grands projets. Par contre, plus que ses confrères il travailla à l'étranger. Dans les années 70, il conçut pour Vitra une nouvelle usine de meubles à Weil am Rhein, dans les années 80, il créa le pavillon britannique pour l'Expo de Séville et, à l'heure actuelle, il achève un bâtiment industriel à Cologne et travaille à un projet pour la nouvelle bourse de Berlin.

La gare de Waterloo est sa plus impressionnante création, une construction harmonieuse, vigoureuse qui se marie

gloomy prospects of many buildings – they could not be leased and remained empty, and their owners as well as a number of architects went bankrupt – but also the fact that British Post-Modern architecture had been closely connected with this boom.

Nicholas Grimshaw was virtually the only architect of his generation who did not manage to participate in the office tower building boom. He has only now slowly begun to receive substantial commissions. Up to this point, he had devoted ever more attention towards architectonic projects outside of Great Britain. In the 1970s he designed a new furniture factory for Vitra in Weil am Rhein, in the 1980s he built the British pavilion at the Seville Expo and he is currently completing a factory building in Cologne and developing a project for a new stock market in Berlin.

The new train station is his most impressive design. The supple, powerful construction nestles against the neighbouring 19th century station. The building's design gives clear indications of the strength and weaknesses of the British High Tech style, with its emphasis upon the labour-intensive installation of different building components by skilled craftsmen. In many countries it is no longer possible to work like this. Their building industries have long since become more efficient by the replacement of skilled craftsmanship with more dependable but also less imaginative prefabricated components.

brachte nicht nur die Bauwerke selbst in Verruf – von denen viele nicht vermietet werden konnten und leerstanden und deren Bauherren einschließlich einiger Architekten bankrott gingen –, sondern auch die britische Postmoderne, die mit diesem Boom in enger Verbindung stand.

Nicholas Grimshaw war beinahe der einzige seiner Generation und seines Berufsstandes, dem es nicht gelang, sich am Bauboom der Bürogebäude zu beteiligen. Erst jetzt befaßt er sich nach und nach mit wirklich großen Bauaufträgen. Dafür engagierte sich Grimshaw in zunehmendem Maße bei architektonischen Projekten im Ausland. In den 70er Jahren entwarf er für Vitra eine neue Möbelfabrik in Weil am Rhein, in den 80er Jahren baute er den britischen Pavillon für die Expo in Sevilla, und zur Zeit vollendet er ein Fabrikgebäude in Köln und arbeitet an einem Projekt für die neue Berliner Börse.

Das neue Bahnhofsgebäude ist der beeindruckendste seiner Entwürfe, eine geschmeidige, kraftvolle Konstruktion, die sich an den benachbarten Bahnhof aus dem 19. Jahrhundert anschmiegt. Das Design dieses Bauwerks zeigt deutlich die Stärken und Schwächen des britischen High-Tech-Stils, bei dem die arbeitsaufwendige handwerkliche Montage verschiedener Bauteile zu einer Tugend erklärt wurde. Eine solche Arbeitsweise wäre in vielen Ländern nicht mehr möglich, weil dort die Bauindustrie dadurch effizienter wurde, daß

très bien à la gare 19ème voisine. La conception de cet édifice montre clairement la force et la faiblesse du style High Tech britannique qui érige au rang de vertu la prouesse technique. Dans bien des pays, où les méthodes anciennes ont été abandonnées au profit d'éléments préfabriqués plus sûrs mais plus banals, un tel travail ne serait plus possible.

Le véritable chant du cygne du boom de la construction à Londres vint justement d'un architecte qui a quitté l'Angleterre depuis cinquante ans, Ralph Erskine. Sur la commande d'un investisseur originaire de Suède, où Erskine vit et travaille depuis plusieurs décennies, il créa à Hammersmith The Ark. Cette arche n'a rien à voir avec les immeubles de bureaux postmodernes de la ville et leur style prétentieux. C'est un exercice plein d'allant, un peu individualiste, mê-

Somewhat surprisingly, the actual swan-song of London's building boom and its special style of building was performed by Ralph Erskine, an architect who had left England fifty years earlier. He was commissioned by an investor in Sweden – where he has lived and worked for decades – to build The Ark in Hammersmith. The building has nothing in common with the pretentious Art deco style of this area's Post-Modern office towers. The resolute, somewhat unconventional design is combined with Scandinavian reticence. The Ark, designed by an architect at the end of his career, is located beside an urban freeway. This self-contained, huge glass egg represents a new definition of an office building. It is still empty.

Zaha Hadid, an Iraqi living in London, is equally unconventional in her designs. She has only recently seen her first building realized: a fire-station for the Vitra company. Hadid's picturesque and extravagant designs have been stimulated by the work of Supremists such as Malevich and El Lissitzky. One of her aims is to baffle and shock.

France

While Great Britain is slowly emerging out of the wreckage of the building boom, France not only has to overcome the ruinous politics of the Mitterrand era but also faces the end of the public funding for the many large projects which radically changed Paris. Towards the end, these projects were ever more de-

man alte Handwerkskünste zugunsten zuverlässiger, aber einfallsloser Fertigbauteile fallen ließ.

Der eigentliche Schwanengesang auf Londons Bauboom und seinen speziellen Baustil war ausgerechnet von einem

lé de réserve scandinave. Œuvre d'un créateur en fin de carrière, l'Arche se trouve près d'une autoroute. Enorme œuf de verre clos, elle donne une définition nouvelle du local professionnel. Local d'ailleurs resté vide.

pendent on the growing investments from the private sector. This was a change, but it allowed for the construction of Paris' largest and newest symbol, Nouvel's so-called Tour Sans Fins (Tower without Boundaries) in La Défense. This highrise is going to be as tall as the World Trade Center in New York City.

It was two British High Tech architects – Richard Rogers and Norman Foster – who revived French architecture in the 1980s, and pulled it out of the stagnation to which it had succumbed after the death of such masters of the Modern Movement as Le Corbusier and Jean Prouvé. The Centre Pompidou (architects: Rogers and Piano) provided a strong stimulation to a latent French interest in exhibitionistic Futurism. Nobody was more successful in imparting

Architekten zu hören, der England vor fünfzig Jahren verlassen hat: Ralph Erskine. Im Auftrag eines Investors aus Schweden, wo er seit Jahrzehnten lebt und arbeitet, baute Erskine in Hammersmith The Ark. Die Arche hat nichts mit dem aufgeblasenen Art-deco-Stil der postmodernen Bürogebäude in der Stadt gemein, sondern ist eine entschlossene, ein wenig eigenwillige Übung in Formgebung, kombiniert mit skandinavischer Zurückhaltung. Die Arche, die von einem Architekten am Ende seiner Karriere entworfen wurde, liegt neben einer Stadtautobahn: ein in sich geschlossenes, riesiges Glasei, eine Neudefinition des Bürogebäudes. Eines, das noch immer leersteht.

Ebenso eigenwillig in ihrer Formgebung ist die in London lebende Irakerin Zaha Hadid, obwohl sie gerade erst mit der Feuerwache für die Fabrik der Firma Vitra ihren ersten Bau verwirklicht hat. Hadids malerische und extravagante Arbeiten suchen ihre Anregungen bei den Suprematisten wie Malewitsch und El Lissitzky und haben immer den Anspruch, verblüffen und schockieren zu wollen.

Frankreich

Während Großbritannien sich langsam aus den Trümmern des Baubooms erhebt, muß Frankreich nicht nur die ruinöse Politik der Ära Mitterrand überwinden, sondern auch das Ende der öffentlichen Finanzierung zahlreicher großer Projekte, die die Stadt Paris radikal verwandelt hätten. Die letzten dieser Bau-

Installée à Londres et tout aussi volontariste dans ses conceptions, l'Irakienne Zaha Hadid vient seulement de réaliser son premier projet en Allemagne, le poste anti-incendie des usines de la firme Vitra. Les travaux de Hadid, extravagants, de type pictural, s'inspirent de suprématistes comme Malevitch et El Lissitsky et cherchent toujours à étonner et à choquer.

La France

Tandis que la Grande Bretagne se relève lentement des ruines du boom, la France doit non seulement surmonter les problèmes dûs à la politique ruineuse de l'ère Mitterrand mais aussi ceux provoqués par la fin du financement public de nombreux grands projets, qui auraient changé radicalement le visage de Paris. Les dernières réalisations avaient fini par se faire grâce à un financement privé de plus en plus important. C'est à cette tendance que l'on doit l'existence de la nouvelle image de marque de la ville, la fameuse Tour Sans Fins de Nouvel dans le quartier de la Défense, un gratte-ciel de la hauteur du World Trade Center à New York.

Ce furent sans doute les architectes High Tech britanniques Richard Rogers et Norman Foster qui, dans les années 80, amorcèrent la revitalisation de l'architecture française. Ils la sortirent de la stagnation dans laquelle elle se trouvait depuis la disparition de maîtres de la modernité comme Le Corbusier et Jean Prouvé. Le Centre Pompidou (architec-

France's High Tech response to England is Jean Nouvel. Left: design for the Galeries Lafayette in Berlin. Below: factory for Cartier in Villeret (Switzerland)

Frankreichs High-Tech-Antwort auf England ist Jean Nouvel. Links: Entwurf für die Galeries Lafayette in Berlin. Unten: Fabrik für den Cartier-Konzern in Villeret (Schweiz)

La réponse française au High Tech britannique, c'est Jean Nouvel. A gauche, projet pour les Galeries Lafayette à Berlin. En bas: usine pour Cartier à Villeret (Suisse)

a French accent to the High Tech style than Jean Nouvel, who once compared his work to the art of making a film.
When one compares Nouvel's Institut du Monde arabe (Institute of the Arab World) in Paris with the new Waterloo Station in London, one immediately is confronted with the difference in the two tendencies within the one school. Grimshaw has created a forum where not even the smallest detail is ignored – right down to the gasket and steel bolt – even if this is sometimes to the detriment of the overall impression. In contrast, Nouvel has a more liberal attitude towards details, as long as the final result is meaningful.

werke waren immer abhängiger von steigenden Investitionen der privaten Wirtschaft geworden – ein Wandel, der dennoch zum Bau von Paris' größtem neuem Wahrzeichen führt: Nouvels sogenanntem Tour Sans Fins (Turm ohne Grenzen) in La Défense, einem Wolkenkratzer von der Höhe des New Yorker World Trade Centers.
Es waren wohl die britischen High-Tech-Architekten Richard Rogers und Norman Foster, die für eine Wiederbelebung der französischen Architektur in den 80er Jahren gesorgt haben. Sie holten sie aus ihrem Zustand der Stagnation, in dem sie sich seit dem Tod der Meister der Moderne wie Le Corbusier

tes: Rogers et Piano) donna un élan notable à l'intérêt latent en France pour un futurisme provocateur. Personne ne sut mieux que Jean Nouvel, qui compara un jour sa méthode de travail à l'art du cinéaste, donner au style High Tech l'accent français.
En comparant l'Institut du Monde arabe, construit à Paris par Nouvel, à la gare de Waterloo, il apparaît immédiatement qu'on est en présence de deux tendances d'une même école: Grimshaw a créé un forum dans lequel la plus grande attention a été accordée au moindre détail – depuis les manchettes de joints jusqu'au boulons d'acier – ce qui, toutefois, nuit parfois à l'impression d'en-

The Netherlands

Although it is a small country, the Netherlands remains one of Europe's most interesting architectural centres. Just as in the glorious days of the 1920s, Holland is once again home to two architectonic movements which would seem to be mutually exclusive. Seventy years ago, the white-walled Purism of J. J. P. Oud (De Stijl) stood in stark contrast to the elaborate brick atavism of the Amsterdam School. Today, a similar break between Calvinism and Catholicism is exemplified in Rem Koolhaas' defiant and picturesque formulation of contemporary Modernism and Aldo van Eyck's sham aestheticism. Younger architects, such as the Mecanoo Group, distinguish themselves through their fascinating ability to link the High Tech image with a more expressive formal repertoire and a greater diversity of materials. It is precisely the comprehensive nature of their work which elicits responses from all over the continent.

The South: Italy and the Ticino

In comparison with other European countries, Italy has seen little building activity during the last decade. And architecture currently plays a weaker public role here than in the past. Only a few municipalities – and no branches of the national government – invest in architecture of a high quality. The themes and aims of different projects are often flogged to death in years of discussion.

und Jean Prouvé befand, heraus. Das Centre Pompidou (Architekten: Rogers und Piano) verlieh dem in Frankreich latent vorhandenen Interesse für exhibitionistischen Futurismus einen kraftvollen Impuls. Niemandem gelang es besser, den High-Tech-Stil mit einem französischen Akzent zu versehen, als Jean Nouvel, der einmal seine Arbeiten mit der Kunst des Filmemachens verglich.

Wenn man Nouvels Institut du Monde arabe (Institut der arabischen Welt) in Paris mit dem neuen Waterloo-Bahnhof vergleicht, erkennt man sofort den Unterschied zwischen zwei Richtungen ein und derselben Schule: Grimshaw hat ein Forum geschaffen, das sich hingebungsvoll auch dem kleinsten Detail – von den Dichtungsmanschetten bis zu den Stahlbolzen – widmet, was manchmal auf Kosten des Gesamteindrucks geht. Dagegen ist Nouvel bereit, bezüglich der Details großzügiger zu verfahren, solange eine aussagekräftige architektonische Form gewährleistet ist.

Die Niederlande

Im Verhältnis zu ihrer Größe sind die Niederlande nach wie vor eines der interessantesten Architekturzentren Europas. Genau wie in den glorreichen Tagen der 20er Jahre ist Holland die Heimat zweier einander offensichtlich ausschließender architektonischer Strömungen. Damals war es der weißwandige Purismus von J. J. P. Oud (De Stijl) im Gegensatz zum verschnörkelten Ziegelstein-Atavismus der Amsterdamer

semble. A l'inverse, Nouvel est prêt à des compromis dans les détails au profit d'une forme architecturale forte.

Les Pays-Bas

Les Pays-Bas sont une petite nation mais aussi un des centres architecturaux les plus intéressants d'Europe. Tout comme ce fut le cas pendant les glorieuses années 20, ce pays abrite deux courants d'inspiration qui, visiblement, s'excluent l'un l'autre. Jadis, le purisme aux murs blancs de J. J. P. Oud (De Stijl) s'opposait à l'atavisme de l'école d'Amsterdam, avec ses décorations de brique sophistiquées. Aujourd'hui, reproduisant pareille scission entre calvinisme et catholicisme, on trouve le modernisme impertinent et pittoresque d'un Rem Koolhaas et le pseudo-esthétisme d'un Aldo van Eyck. Des architectes plus jeunes, comme ceux du groupe Mecanoo, se caractérisent par une extraordinaire faculté d'enrichir le style High Tech d'un répertoire formel plus expressif et d'une palette technique plus diversifiée. Et cet élargissement a des résonnances dans tout le continent.

Le Sud: l'Italie et le Tessin

On a assez peu construit en Italie durant la dernière décennie et, par conséquent, le rôle de l'architecture a diminué dans ce pays. Bien peu de municipalités – et certainement aucune instance de l'Etat – investissent dans des réalisations de qualité. Bien des idées, bien des projets

Competitions for public buildings are very rare and are virtually unheard of for private buildings. Exhibitions and similar events are often only concerned with making an impression, for example, that they actually provide younger architects with the opportunity to build.

The most important Italian architects often work abroad, where they are not understood as representatives of Italian architecture but rather as individuals. They build in other countries. In Italy they edit a magazine or teach at a university. The universities, however, have lost touch with reality and have thereby relinquished a great deal of their former influence. At one time they played major roles in the revival of historic inner cities and of architectural regionalism.

Before Renzo Piano – who was born in Genoa in 1937 – could build the Col-

In the Ticino Mario Botta is »primus inter pares« and no longer builds only single-family houses: administration building in Bellinzona

Mario Botta ist im Tessin der »Primus inter pares« und baut nicht mehr nur Einfamilienhäuser: Verwaltungsgebäude in Bellinzona

Prophète en son pays, le Tessin, Mario Botta ne construit plus seulement des maisons individuelles: locaux administratifs à Bellinzona

Schule. Heute, in einem ähnlichen Bruch zwischen Kalvinismus und Katholizismus, gibt es den trotzigen und pittoresken Modernismus der Gegenwart eines Rem Koolhaas und den Scheinästhetizismus eines Aldo van Eyck. Jüngere Architekten wie die Gruppe Mecanoo zeichnen sich durch die faszinierende Fähigkeit aus, das Bild des High-Tech mit einem ausdrucksstärkeren formalen Repertoire und einer vielseitigeren Materialpalette zu verknüpfen. Und es ist diese Einschließlichkeit, die ihr Echo auf dem gesamten Kontinent findet.

Der Süden: Italien und Tessin

In Italien wurde im letzten Jahrzehnt vergleichsweise wenig gebaut, und die Architektur spielt deswegen zur Zeit eine geringere öffentliche Rolle, als wir es von Italien gewohnt sind. Nur wenige Stadtverwaltungen – und schon gar nicht die staatlichen Behörden – investieren in qualitativ hochstehender Architektur. Viele Themen und Aufgaben werden in jahrelangen Diskussionen zerredet. Wettbewerbe sind für öffentliche Bauten sehr selten und für private fast undenkbar. Ausstellungen und Veranstaltungen erwecken oft nur den Anschein, jüngeren Architekten die Möglichkeit zum Bauen zu eröffnen.

Die bedeutenden italienischen Architekten arbeiten häufig im Ausland. Dort werden sie aber nicht als Vertreter einer italienischen Architektur angesehen, sondern als Individuen. Im Ausland bauen sie, in Italien geben sie eine Zeit-

disparaissent, à force d'être discutés, des années durant. Si des concours pour la construction de bâtiments publics sont très rares, pour des bâtiments privés, ils sont presque inconcevables. Expositions et manifestations donnent souvent l'impression, illusoire, d'offrir des possibilités de travail à de jeunes architectes.

Les grands architectes italiens travaillent souvent à l'étranger. On les perçoit cependant en tant qu'individus et non comme représentants d'une architecture italienne. A l'étranger, ils construisent et, en Italie, ils publient un magazine ou donnent des cours à l'université. Seulement, justement, les écoles spécialisées ont perdu le contact avec la réalité et leur influence s'en trouve d'autant affaiblie alors que jadis, elles étaient en position de redonner vie aux quartiers historiques des villes ou de susciter une culture architecturale régionale.

Avant que Renzo Piano, né à Gênes en 1937, ne pût construire le stade de Bari, il avait gagné la plupart de ses galons à l'étranger (Centre Pompidou, Menil Collection à Houston, Texas). En 1989, il gagna le concours pour la construction de l'aéroport d'Osaka, en cours de réalisation sur une île de la baie et, en 1991, le concours de la Potsdamer Platz.

Aldo Rossi travaille en France, en Allemagne, en Angleterre et au Japon. Peut-être est-ce la raison pour laquelle son œuvre n'étouffe pas dans un carcan stylistique, comme on aurait pu le craindre, mais qu'il trouve des solutions plus abs-

umbus exhibition in his hometown and the football stadium in Bari, he received most of his plaudits from abroad (Centre Pompidou, Menil Collection in Houston, Texas). In 1989 he won the competition for the airport in Osaka – currently being realized on an offshore island in the bay – and in 1991 he won the competition for Potsdamer Platz. Aldo Rossi has built in France, Germany, England and Japan, and this is perhaps a reason why he has been able to avoid an early threat to his work: the danger of suffocation in a uniform style of archetypal forms. Instead, Rossi has arrived at more abstract solutions, such as the Hotel Il Palazzo in Fukuoka, Japan or his Bonnefanten Museum in Maastricht. In comparison with these architects, Gino Valle does a great deal of work in Italy. He too, however, cannot be understood as a repre-

schrift heraus oder unterrichten an den Universitäten. Allerdings haben gerade die Hochschulen den Kontakt zur Realität und entsprechend ihren Einfluß verloren, wo sie früher die Revitalisierung der historischen Stadtkerne oder auch eine regionalistische Architekturkultur forcieren konnten.

Bevor der 1937 in Genua geborene Renzo Piano für die Columbus-Ausstellung in seiner Heimatstadt und das Fußballstadion in Bari bauen konnte, hatte er seine Meriten überwiegend im Ausland verdient (Centre Pompidou, Menil Collection in Houston, Texas). 1989 gewann er den Wettbewerb für den Bau des Flughafens von Osaka, der zur Zeit auf einer vorgelagerten Insel in der Bucht realisiert wird, und 1991 jenen für den Potsdamer Platz.

Aldo Rossi baut in Frankreich, Deutsch-

traites comme le prouvent l'hôtel Il Palazzo, à Fukuoka, au Japon ou son Musée Bonnefant, à Maastricht.

Gino Valle, par comparaison à Rossi, travaille beaucoup dans son pays. Mais on ne peut non plus lui attribuer un style proprement italien ni noter chez lui de thèmes récurrents.

D'autres architectes italiens de valeur, le Florentin Adolfo Natalini, le Romain Francesco Cellini et le Napolitain Francesco Venezia n'ont que rarement l'occasion de réaliser concrètement leurs projets. Le travail raffiné de Natalini pour le nouveau théâtre de Rimini ou l'idée de Cellini pour le pavillon italien de la Biennale de Venise n'existent jusqu'à présent que sur le papier.

En réaction au pluralisme chaotique de l'architecture contemporaine en Italie (tel qu'il apparut lors de la Biennale) une tendance se fait jour qui tente de s'opposer à l'anarchie stylistique par une simplification des moyens formels. Les représentants de ce «minimalisme» italien sont Giorgio Grassi, Antonio Monestiroli et Franco Stella. Malheureusement, en Italie, les exemples concrets n'abondent pas. A Groningen, en Hollande, se trouve l'œuvre la plus importante à ce jour de Grassi, une bibliothèque municipale qui date de 1992.

La qualité particulière de l'architecture italienne moderne réside dans les rapports qu'elle entretient avec l'environnement historique. Ces dernières années on a développé dans ce pays des méthodes et des techniques destinées

Gino Valle and Aldo Rossi can be counted amongst Italy's superstars. Left: disciplined housing in Venice (Valle). Below: Rossi's typical design sketches – here for the Bonnefantenmuseum in Maastricht (NL)

Gino Valle und Aldo Rossi zählen zu den italienischen Superstars. Links: disziplinierter Wohnungsbau in Venedig (Gino Valle). Unten: Rossis typische Entwurfsskizzen – hier für das Bonnefantenmuseum in Maastricht

Gino Valle et Aldo Rossi font partie des superstars de l'architecture italienne. A gauche: style rigoureux pour un immeuble d'appartements à Venise (Gino Valle). En bas: esquisses typiques de Rossi – ici pour le Musée Bonnefant de Maastricht (Pays-Bas)

sentative of a particularly Italian style, nor can one detect any recurrent themes in his work.

Other talented Italian architects, such as Adolfo Natalini from Florence, Francesco Cellini from Rome and Francesco Venezi from Naples are seldom given a chance to realize their designs. Natalini's ingenious design for the new theatre in Rimini and Cellini's idea for the new Italian pavilion for the Biennale in Venice are still only on paper.

land, England und Japan. Vielleicht ist das der Grund dafür, daß Rossis Arbeit nicht in einem einheitlichen Stil aus archetypischen Formen erstickt, wie es zu befürchten war, sondern er zu abstrakteren Lösungen kommt, wie das Hotel Il Palazzo in Fukuoka, Japan, oder sein Bonnefantenmuseum in Maastricht beweisen.

Gino Valle arbeitet vergleichsweise häufig in Italien. Aber auch an ihm kann man keinen eigentlich italienischen Stil fest-

à la conservation et la restauration de monuments. Dans le cas de constructions neuves situées dans un contexte historique, on a toujours veillé à une insertion respectueuse dans l'environnement immédiat.

Massimo Carmassi, Pasquale Culotta ou Guido Canali ont montré une grande sensibilité dans l'exercice de cette spécialité. Ils ne cherchent pas à recréer ce qui s'est perdu mais souhaitent concilier caractère original et nouveauté.

There has also been a reaction against the chaotic pluralism of contemporary Italian architecture (as presented at the Biennale). It has tended to counter stylistic anarchy with the reduction of formal methods. This new Italian »Minimalism« is represented by Giorgio Grassi, Antonio Monestiroli and Franco Stella. Unfortunately, there is no built example of this within Italy. Grassi's most important building, completed in 1992, is the Municipal Library in Groningen (Netherlands).

The real value of contemporary, realized Italian architecture lies in its relationship to its historical environment. In recent years, appropriate methods and techniques for the conservation and restoration of historical monuments have been developed in Italy. Moreover, when a new building is placed directly within a

machen, auch bei ihm sind keine wiederkehrenden Themen erkennbar.

Andere begabte italienische Architekten, wie der Florentiner Adolfo Natalini, der Römer Francesco Cellini und der Neapoletaner Francesco Venezia, bekommen nur selten die Chance, ihre Entwürfe zu realisieren. Natalinis raffinierter Entwurf für das neue Theater in Rimini oder Cellinis Idee für den neuen italienischen Pavillon auf der Biennale in Venedig gibt es bisher nur auf Papier.

Als Reaktion auf den chaotischen Pluralismus der zeitgenössischen Architektur in Italien (wie er sich auf der Biennale präsentierte) ist allerdings eine Tendenz zu erkennen, bei der durch Reduktion der formalen Mittel versucht wird, sich einer stilistischen Anarchie entgegenzustellen. Für diesen italienischen »Minimalismus« stehen Giorgio Grassi, Antonio Monestiroli und Franco Stella. Leider fehlt der gebaute Beweis innerhalb Italiens. Im niederländischen Groningen steht Grassis bisher bedeutendstes Werk, die Stadtbibliothek von 1992.

Die eigentliche Qualität der gegenwärtigen gebauten italienischen Architektur liegt in ihrem Umgang mit ihrer historischen Umgebung. In den letzten Jahren wurden in Italien geeignete Methoden und Techniken für die Konservierung und Restaurierung von Baudenkmälern entwickelt. Aber auch im Neubau in historischer Umgebung wurde immer auf respektvolle Einfügung geachtet.

Massimo Carmassi, Pasquale Culotta und Guido Canali haben sich dabei als

Les rapports de l'architecture nouvelle avec la tradition ont dépassé tout formalisme pour entamer un dialogue constructif. C'est ce que prouvent les projets pour des églises de Augusto Romano Burelli et le projet de Paolo Portoghesi et de Vittorio Gigliotti pour la nouvelle mosquée de Rome. La construction d'une mosquée et d'un centre islamique dans la capitale du catholicisme n'a pas pour but de créer un nouveau type d'édifice mais plutôt de diversifier les constructions islamiques traditionnelles.

Au Tessin aussi, on parle italien. L'architecture tessinoise a une place de choix dans le paysage européen, bien que son territoire soit très exigu. La situation de cette région au croisement de cultures diverses, ajoutée à un développement économique positif ont fait qu'un groupe assez homogène d'architectes de talent s'y est formé. L'architecture des formes pures pratiquée par Mario Botta pour ses villas et une utilisation nouvelle de matériaux locaux furent, au début des années 80, un véritable événement sur la scène architecturale. Aujourd'hui encore, cet architecte applique les mêmes règles et principes de composition à des projets plus vastes, comme la banca Gottardo, à Lugano.

Outre Botta, un autre noyau d'architectes de valeur est en activité: Ivano Gianola, Bruno Reichlin et Fabio Reinhart, Luigi Snozzi, Livio Vacchini et Aurelio Galfetti. On leur doit la médiathèque de Chambéry ou encore un projet de concours pour un centre culturel en Nouvel-

Left: Italy – Massimo Carmassi, San Michele in Borgo. Below: Rafael Moneo's new airport in Seville (Spain), wall detail

Links: Massimo Carmassi, San Michele in Borgo (Italien). Unten: Rafael Moneos neuer Flughafen in Sevilla, Wanddetail

A gauche: Massimo Carmassi, San Michele à Borgo (Italie). En bas: le nouvel aérodrome de Séville par Rafael Moneo, détail d'un mur, Espagne

Architectural tasks for Spain in the 1990s: new train stations for a better infra-structure. Below: Attocha train station in Madrid (Rafael Moneo). Right: Santa Justa train station in Seville, detail (Cruz and Ortiz)

Spanische Bauaufgaben der 90er Jahre: neue Bahnhöfe für eine bessere Infrastruktur. Unten: Bahnhof Attocha in Madrid (Rafael Moneo); rechts: Bahnhof Santa Justa in Sevilla, Detail (Cruz und Ortiz)

Grands travaux des années 90 en Espagne: gares nouvelles pour une meilleure infra-structure. En bas: gare Attocha à Madrid (Rafael Moneo); à droite: gare Santa Justa à Séville, détail (Cruz et Ortiz)

historical environment, a great deal of care is taken to ensure that it fits in properly.

Massimo Carmassi, Pasquale Culotta and Guido Canali have shown themselves to be particularly adept in this respect. Although they do not attempt to restore what has been lost and ascribe an independence to the new construction, they also want to preserve the original character of the historical context.

The relationship of Italy's new architecture to tradition has now overcome its formalistic tendencies. A constructive dialogue with the architectural tradition is taking place, as is exemplified in Augusto Romano Burelli's church projects and in the new design by Paolo Portog-

besonders sensibel erwiesen. Sie versuchen nicht, Verlorenes wiederherzustellen, jedoch möchten sie auf den ursprünglichen Charakter bei gleichzeitiger Eigenständigkeit nicht verzichten.

Die Beziehung der neuen Architektur zur Tradition hat ihren formalistischen Charakter überwunden, um einen konstruktiven Dialog mit der Bautradition einzugehen. Das bezeugen die Kirchenprojekte von Augusto Romano Burelli und der Entwurf für die Moschee in Rom von Paolo Portoghesi und Vittorio Gigliotti. Mit der Moschee und dem islamischen Zentrum in der Hauptstadt des Katholizismus wird kein neuer Bautypus erfunden, sondern traditionelle islamische Bauweisen werden variiert.

le-Calédonie, deux exemples dans lesquels le rôle de l'architecture et ses rapports avec le paysage naturel ou urbain sont mis en exergue. Le travail de Luigi Snozzi est une prise de position contre le viol et le morcellement du paysage, et tente simultanément d'échapper au formalisme envahissant de l'époque contemporaine.

L'Espagne et le Portugal

Juste après la fin du franquisme, beaucoup d'architectes espagnols, dans leur recherche d'un langage nouveau, s'étaient montrés plus proches des architectes modernes de l'époque classique que de leurs confrères européens et américains. Leur désir était d'exprimer

hesi and Vittorio Gigliotti for the new mosque in Rome. Far from being an attempt to develop a new type of building, this mosque and Islamic centre in the capital city of Catholicism represents variations on traditional Islamic architecture.

In Ticino Italian is spoken too, but despite the fact that this region covers a very small area, its architecture occupies a prominent position in the European architectural panorama. Its geographic location at a juncture of different cultures as well as its consistently positive economic development have contributed to the formation of a rather homogeneous group of talented architects. Mario Botta's villa architecture of pure forms and his new ways of using conventional building materials caused quite a stir in the architectural scene in the early 1980s. He has now applied the same compositional rules and principles to larger projects, such as the Banca del Gottardo in Lugano.

Apart from Botta, a small group of important architects is also active in Ticino. It includes Ivano Gianola, Bruno Reichlin and Fabio Reinhart, Luigi Snozzi, Livio Vacchini and Aurelio Galfetti.

The latter's work includes the mediatheque in Chambéry and a competition design for a cultural centre in New Caledonia, in which the role of architecture and its relationship to the landscape and to the city is given confident emphasis. In contrast, while avoiding the effusive formalism of many contemporary archi-

Auch im Tessin spricht man italienisch. Und die Tessiner Architektur hat im europäischen Architekturpanorama eine herausragende Stellung, obwohl die Region selbst flächenmäßig sehr klein ist. Die geographische Lage am Kreuzungspunkt verschiedener Kulturen hat zusammen mit einer stets positiven wirtschaftlichen Entwicklung dazu beigetragen, daß sich im Tessin eine recht homogene Gruppe talentierter Architekten gebildet hat. Mario Bottas Villenarchitektur der reinen Formen und die neuartige Nutzung herkömmlicher Baumaterialien waren Anfang der 80er Jahre ein wahres Ereignis für die Architekturszene. Die gleichen Kompositionsregeln und -prinzipien hat er jetzt auch bei größeren Projekten wie der Banca del Gottardo in Lugano angewandt.

Außer Botta ist noch eine kleinere Gruppe weiterer bedeutender Architekten tätig: Ivano Gianola, Bruno Reichlin und Fabio Reinhart, Luigi Snozzi, Livio Vacchini und Aurelio Galfetti.

Von letztgenanntem stammen die Mediathek in Chambéry und ein Wettbewerbsentwurf für ein Kulturzentrum in Neukaledonien, bei denen die Rolle der Architektur und die Beziehung zur Landschaft oder zur Stadt mit Zuversicht unterstrichen werden. Die Arbeit von Luigi Snozzi bezieht hingegen schon einmal bewußt gegen die geschundene und zersiedelte Landschaft Stellung, versucht sich dabei aber dem überschwenglichen Formalismus vieler gegenwärtiger Architekten zu entziehen.

l'optimisme et la confiance. Ils refusaient le déconstructivisme et le postmodernisme moribond comme étant des attitudes intellectuelles négatives. Toute tendance impliquant doute, critique ou défiance était vouée à l'échec. C'est l'architecture européenne des années 30 qui semblait la plus apte à permettre une vision optimiste de l'avenir. L'architecture espagnole se trouve à présent dans la seconde phase du post-franquisme. A ses débuts, peu de créateurs possédaient l'autorité nécessaire pour représenter la jeune démocratie. Puis, l'Exposition de Séville, les Jeux Olympiques de Barcelone et un flot de commandes publiques donnèrent leur chance à la jeune génération d'architectes.

C'était une chance exceptionnelle: il fallait réaliser en un temps très court des aérodromes, des gares, des bâtiments

tects, at times, Luigi Snozzi's work has deliberately avoided the exploited and over-developed landscape.

Spain and Portugal

In the years immediately after the end of the Franco regime, many Spanish architects who were searching for a new vocabulary of forms did not look to contemporary European or American architecture but rather to the classic Modern Movement. Spanish architects wanted to lend expression to optimism and confidence. Deconstructivism and a waning Post-Modernism were rejected as intellectual positions. Architectural tendencies which showed signs of doubt, criticism and mistrust had little chance of acceptance. European architecture of the 1930s seemed much

Spanien und Portugal

Unmittelbar nach Ende des Franco-Regimes hatten sich viele spanische Architekten auf der Suche nach einer neuen Formensprache weniger an der zeitgenössischen europäischen oder amerikanischen Architektur orientiert, sondern eher an der klassischen Moderne. Die spanischen Architekten wollten Optimismus und Zuversicht zum Ausdruck bringen. Dekonstruktivismus und der dahinscheidende Postmodernismus wurden als intellektualisierte Haltungen abgelehnt. Alle Tendenzen, die Zweifel, Kritik und Mißtrauen aufwiesen, konnten nicht Fuß fassen. Besser geeignet für die Umsetzung eines hoffnungsvollen Blicks in die Zukunft erschien die europäische Architektur der 30er Jahre. Inzwischen befindet sich die spanische

administratifs et culturels. La construction locative cherchait de nouveaux emplacements et les Jeux provoquèrent par exemple la création de toutes pièces d'un nouveau quartier en prolongement sud du vieux quadrillage de la Cerdà. Si le gros du projet fut l'œuvre de l'agence la plus influente de Barcelone, Martorell, Bohigas, Mackay, de jeunes architectes en réalisèrent les maisons.

De vastes échanges eurent lieu entre constructeurs nationaux et internationaux et même le style d'une personnalité aussi considérable que Rafael Moneo s'en trouva influencé. Son projet pour un nouveau Palais du festival à Venise ou son musée Miró, à Palma de Majorque, récemment inauguré, ont trouvé une dimension internationale tout en tenant compte, comme par le passé, de l'implantation, du paysage et du climat. Cela est vrai aussi pour le nouvel aérodrome de Séville, dont il est l'auteur.

Quelques faits marquants: le travail du couple d'architectes Enric Miralles et Carme Pinós se confond avec le monde de la sculpture. Leur cimetière d'Igualda, à Barcelone, s'insère dans les collines du paysage comme une longue et sinueuse plastique. Juan Navarro Baldeweg continue de s'interroger sur l'intérêt des leitmotive dans le langage formel de l'architecture. Chez ce créateur de Santander, le thème de la coupole aérienne est une véritable «obsession», qui est un fil directeur de tous ses projets et trouve sa plus belle réalisation dans le palais des congrès, à Salamanca.

more appropriate to the articulation of
hopes for the future.

In the interim, Spanish architecture has
entered into the second post-Franco
phase. Initially, only a few architects
were actively involved by the state in
the presentation of the new democracy,
but the Seville Expo, the Olympic
Games in Barcelona and a flood of public commissions gave a younger generation of architects their chance.

It was a unique opportunity. Within a
short amount of time airports, train stations and administrative and cultural
centres had to be built. A new approach
had to be taken to housing. For
example, as a result of the Olympic
Games in Barcelona, an entirely new
district was built. It was constructed as
a continuation of the southern part of
the old Cerdà grid. The master plan for
this district was provided by Bacelona's
most influential architectural firm, that
of Martorell, Bohigas and Mackay. A
number of Spain's younger architects
designed houses for this district.

This was a time of far-reaching ex-
changes between national and international architects. In the process, even
the architecture of such an important
figure as Rafael Moneo underwent
changes. His modern design for a new
film palace on the Lido in Venice and his
recently inaugurated Miró museum in
Palma de Mallorca have become more
international, even if considerations of
location, landscape and climate continue to play important roles in his work.

Spain has room for experiments. Below:
Santiago Calatrava's first large – and most
famous – bridge, Bach de Roda in Barcelona. Right: Igualada cemetery near Barcelona (Miralles y Pinós)

Spanien hat Raum für Experimente. Unten:
Santiago Calatravas erste größere, aber
auch berühmteste Brücke, Bach de Roda in
Barcelona. Rechts: Friedhof Igualada bei
Barcelona (Miralles y Pinós)

Le vaste territoire de l'Espagne se prête
aux expériences architecturales. En bas: le
premier grand pont – et aussi le plus célè-
bre – de Santiago Calatrava, Bach de Roda,
à Barcelone. A droite: cimetière Igualada
près de Barcelone (Miralles y Pinós)

The same is true of his new airport in Seville.

Some recent projects are particularly noteworthy. The work of Enric Miralles and Carme Pinós has a close affinity to contemporary sculpture. Their Igualada cemetery in Barcelona stretches like a long, curved sculpture over the hills. Juan Navarro Baldeweg's work pursues the validity of recurring themes in the use of architectonic forms. For this architect from Santander, the motif of the suspended dome has become a veritable obsession, which runs like a thread through his designs. He has used it most effectively in his design for the congress hall in Salamanca. Guillerme Vasquez Consuegra continues in the tradition of the Modern Movement. His housing projects in Cádiz, Seville and Madrid can be understood as constructive criticism of the modern, bleak subsidized housing that can be found on the peripheries of all Spanish cities. In Seville, Antonio Cruz and Antonio Ortiz developed a heroic but still comprehensible interpretation of an urban train station. Finally, with their telephone exchange in the Olympic village, Jaume Bach and Gabriel Mora have shown how one can strike new tones with the strongly contrasting use of forms.

The architect and engineer, Santiago Calatrava, who was born in Valencia, occupies a special position. His complex structures leave the impression that they are based on the skeletal construction of animals. This leads to the conclu-

Architektur in der zweiten Phase nach Franco. Anfänglich waren nur wenige Architekten »staatstragend« bei der Darstellung der neuen Demokratie. Die Expo in Sevilla, die Olympischen Spiele in Barcelona und eine Flut von öffentlichen Aufträgen gaben dann der jüngeren Architektengeneration eine Chance. Es war eine einmalige Chance, denn es mußten Flughäfen, Bahnhöfe, Verwaltungs- und Kulturbauten innerhalb kürzester Zeit realisiert werden. Der Wohnungsbau suchte neue Ansätze; infolge von Olympia wurde beispielsweise ein ganz neuer Stadtteil als südliche Fortsetzung des alten Cerdà-Rasters aus dem Boden gestampft. Den Masterplan lieferte das wohl einflußreichste Büro in Barcelona, Martorell, Bohigas, Mackay; viele jüngere spanische Architekten entwarfen die Häuser.

Es gab einen breit angelegten Austausch zwischen nationalen und internationalen Architekten, und selbst eine so bedeutende Figur wie Rafael Moneo hat sich mit seiner Architektur in diesem Sog verändert. Sein moderner Entwurf für einen neuen Filmpalast in Venedig auf dem Lido und sein jüngst eingeweihtes Miró-Museum in Palma de Mallorca sind internationaler geworden, berücksichtigen aber nach wie vor Ort, Landschaft und Klima. Das gilt auch für seinen neuen Flughafen in Sevilla.

Einige Spotlights: Die Arbeit von Enric Miralles und Carme Pinós schließt sich kurz mit gegenwärtiger Bildhauerei. Ihr Friedhof Igualada in Barcelona fügt sich

Taking unusual paths. Below: congress hall under a suspended dome in Salamanca (Navarro Baldeweg). Right: Fundació Tàpies in Barcelona (Roser Amadó and Lluis Domènech Girbau)

Außergewöhnliche Wege gehen. Unten: Kongreßhalle unter schwebender Kuppel in Salamanca (Navarro Baldeweg). Rechts: Fundació Tàpies in Barcelona (Roser Amadó und Lluis Domènech Girbau)

Démarches originales. En bas: salle des congrès sous une coupole flottante à Salamanca (Navarro Baldeweg). A droite: Fundació Tàpies à Barcelone (Roser Amado et Lluis Domènech Girbau)

sion that it is not only the strength and size of a support which is decisive for its load-bearing capacity, but also its form.

In the small country of Portugal, Alvaro Siza – a Pritzker Prize recipient – is indisputably in a category of his own. This architect from Porto has managed to develop a personal style which takes up the traditions of the Modern Movement, while still maintaining a distanced regionalism. Siza's design for a new building involves a constant process of additions – and of subsequent simplification. This occurred, for example, with his designs for a new building for the faculty of architecture at the University of Porto and for a university in Setubal. Siza's interior spaces are never conceived as static boxes but rather as dynamic spaces, where sloping walls, broken

wie eine lange, geschwungene Plastik in die Hügel. Juan Navarro Baldeweg verfolgt die Gültigkeit von wiederkehrenden Themen der architektonischen Formsprache. Eine wahre »Obsession« ist bei diesem Architekten aus Santander das Motiv der schwebenden Kuppel, das wie ein roter Faden seine Entwürfe durchzieht und in der Kongreßhalle von Salamanca die bisher schönste Anwendung fand.

Guillerme Vasquez Consuegra führt die Tradition der Moderne fort. Mit seinen Wohnungsbauprojekten für Cádiz, Sevilla und Madrid übt er konstruktive Kritik am modernen und trostlosen sozialen Wohnungsbau an der Peripherie der spanischen Großstädte. Antonio Cruz und Antonio Ortiz fanden eine heroische und trotzdem verständliche Interpretation für einen Großstadtbahnhof in Sevilla. Und Jaume Bach und Gabriel Mora haben spätestens seit dem Bau ihrer Telefonzentrale im olympischen Viertel bewiesen, wie man mit einem kontrastreichen Spiel der Formen Akzente setzt.

Eine Sonderstellung mag der in Valencia geborene Architekt und Ingenieur Santiago Calatrava einnehmen. Seine komplexen Strukturen scheinen nach einer aufmerksamen Beobachtung der Skelettkonstruktion von Tieren zu entstehen. Aus dieser Betrachtung folgt die Auffassung, daß nicht nur die Stärke oder Größe einer Stütze für die Tragfähigkeit ausschlaggebend ist, sondern die Form der tragenden Elemente ebenso wichtig ist.

Guillerme Vasquez Consuegra poursuit la tradition moderne. Ses projets de logements pour Cádiz, Séville et Madrid sont une façon positive de critiquer la tristesse de la construction sociale telle qu'on la pratique de nos jours à la périphérie des grandes villes. Antonio Cruz et Antonio Ortiz ont trouvé une interprétation héroïque, et néanmoins compréhensible, pour la construction d'une gare centrale, à Séville. Et enfin, Jaume Bach et Gabriel Mora ont montré depuis leur centrale téléphonique du quartier olympique, comment on crée l'originalité grâce à un jeu de contrastes formels. On peut attribuer une place à part à l'architecte et ingénieur Santiago Calavatra, originaire de Valence. On observe que les formes complexes qu'il crée sem-

wall expanses, proportion and light constantly result in new solutions.

Apart from Alvaro Siza, international recognition has also been obtained by Fernando Távora and Alcino Southino, and by the younger architects, Eduardo Souto de Moura and Gonçalo Byrne. In recent years Fernando Távora has concerned himself with the restoration and extension of historical buildings. Two monasteries, Refóios in Ponte de Lima and Santa Marinha da Costa in Guimarães, are being carefully restored but their extensions tend more towards contrast than continuity. Born in 1952 in Porto, Eduardo Souto de Moura was awarded Portugal's national architectural prize in 1992 for two of his new buildings. His single-family homes are par-

Im kleinen Portugal ist die Ausnahmestellung des Pritzker-Preisträgers Alvaro Siza unbestritten. Dem Architekten aus Porto ist es gelungen, einen persönlichen Stil zu entwickeln, bei dem Traditionen der Moderne aufgegriffen werden und der in einer distanzierten Weise regional ist. Das Entwerfen eines Neubaus wird bei Siza zur ständigen Arbeit des Hinzufügens – und des anschließenden Vereinfachens, wie zum Beispiel bei der neuen Architekturfakultät der Universität von Porto und einer Hochschule in Setubal. Sizas Innenräume werden nie als statische Schachtel gedacht, sondern als dynamische Räume, in denen Licht, Proportion, Durchbrechung und Neigung von Wänden zu immer neuen Lösungen führen.

Neben Alvaro Siza haben inzwischen Fernando Távora und Alcino Southino und – von der jüngeren Generation – Eduardo Souto de Moura und Gonçalo Byrne internationale Anerkennung gefunden. Fernando Távora hat sich in den letzten Jahren mit der Restaurierung und Erweiterung von historischer Bausubstanz beschäftigt. Die Klöster Refóios in Ponte de Lima und Santa Marinha da Costa in Guimarães wurden sorgfältig restauriert. Alle Erweiterungen leben jedoch eher vom Kontrast als von der Kontinuität. Der 1952 in Porto geborene Eduardo Souto de Moura hat 1992 für zwei Neubauten den Nationalen Architekturpreis erhalten. Besonders interessant sind seine Einfamilienhäuser, für die eine einfache Grundrißgestaltung

blent découler de la structure du squelette. On peut en conclure que la solidité d'un édifice dépend tout autant de la résistance ou de la taille de la structure que de sa forme.

Dans ce petit pays qu'est le Portugal on s'accorde à dire que le lauréat du prix Pritzker, Alvaro Siza, est un cas exceptionnel. Cet architecte de Porto a réussi à développer un style personnel qui concilie les traditions modernistes et un régionalisme de bon aloi. Lorsqu'il travaille au projet d'un immeuble, Siza procède par ajouts, puis pas simplification. Exemples de cette méthode: l'université de Porto ou une école technique à Setubal. Chez Siza, les intérieurs ne sont jamais des boîtes inertes mais des espaces dynamiques dans lesquels la lumière, la proportion, le cloisonnement et l'inclinaison des murs amènent des solutions toujours nouvelles.

Actuellement, à côté d'Alvaro Siza, Fernando Tàvora et Alcino Southino, ainsi que les jeunes créateurs Eduardo Souto de Moura et Gonçalo Byrne, ont obtenu une réputaion internationale. Ces dernières années, Fernando Tàvora s'est occupé de la restauration du patrimoine historique. Ce fut le cas des cloîtres de Refóios, à Ponte de Lima et de Santa Marinha da Costa, à Guimarães. Par contre, l'intérêt de tous les agrandissements réside plus dans l'effet de contraste que dans celui de continuité. Eduardo Souto de Moura, né à Porto en 1952, a reçu le prix national d'architecture en 1992 pour deux édifices nou-

ticularly interesting, for they are characterized by both simple ground plans and a typically southern European interaction between inner and exterior spaces.

Concluding Remarks

European architecture is an architecture of regions. This means that the scope of the building activity, as well as the approaches taken, are still strongly determined by the socio-economic situations in the individual countries. A few regions – mentioned here in passing or not at all – are still waiting to be connected. In the northern European countries a style of building exists which is invigorating and exemplary, yet the motto here could also read »All quiet on the northern front«. In eastern Europe some time will still have to pass before basic problems – above all, the housing shortage – are resolved. Nevertheless, in the Baltic countries, for example, one can see the first modest attempts at new architectural approaches which are also interesting in formal terms. The »new modesty« is perhaps the common denominator for contemporary European architecture. At the very least, it has toned down and become more subdued than in the hedonistic, animated years of the previous decade.

One further thing: new, confusing terms and labels are of no use. Neither »Dirty Realism« nor a »new architecture of morals« (taken from »Europäische Architektur seit 1968«) does justice to the European patchwork. And that is the way it should be.

mit einer südländischen Durchdringung von Innen und Außen bezeichnend ist.

Schlußbemerkung

Die europäische Architektur lebt vom Europa der Regionen. Das heißt: Auftragsvolumina und auch Denkweisen reflektieren immer noch sehr stark die sozioökonomische Situation der jeweiligen Länder. Einige Regionen – sie werden in diesem Buch nur peripher oder gar nicht erwähnt – warten auf den Anschluß. Im Norden existiert in allen Ländern eine frische vorbildliche Art zu bauen, allerdings nach dem Motto: »Im Norden nichts Neues«. Im Osten wird man noch eine geraume Zeit benötigen, um Grundsatzprobleme, also die Wohnungsnot, zu lösen. Aber es gibt beispielsweise im Baltikum schon bescheidene und formal interessante Architekturansätze dazu.

»Neue Bescheidenheit« ist vielleicht auch der gemeinsame Nenner der aktuellen europäischen Architektur – zumindest ist sie um einige Töne leiser und sanfter geworden als in den hedonistischen, aufbrausenden 80er Jahren.

Und noch eines: Mit neuen verwirrenden Bezeichnungen und Etiketten können wir nicht dienen. Denn weder ein »dirty realism« noch eine »neue Architektur der Moral« (Zitat »Europäische Architektur seit 1968«) können dem europäischen Patchwork gerecht werden. Und das ist auch gut so.

veaux. Ses petites maisons individuelles sont intéressantes et se caractérisent par un plan simple et une interaction de l'intérieur et de l'extérieur.

Conclusion

L'architecture européenne vit de sa diversité: l'abondance des commandes, de même que les mentalités, sont toujours les reflets fidèles de la situation socio-économique des différents pays. Un certain nombre de régions – qui, dans ce livre, sont citées de façon allusive ou pas du tout – attendent leur éveil. Au Nord, on trouve dans tous les pays, un style de construction gai, réussi mais qui, par contre, a pour devise «au nord, rien de nouveau». A l'Est, il faudra encore du temps pour que des problèmes de fond, autrement dit, le manque de logements, soient résolus. Mais on trouve, dans les pays de la Baltique, par exemple, les premiers signes d'une architecture modeste et intéressante. «Nouvelle humilité» est l'expression qui pourrait servir à l'ensemble de l'architecture européenne actuelle – elle est en tout cas devenue bien plus discrète qu'à l'époque hédoniste des années 80. Ajoutons encore ceci: ce n'est pas avec des appellations ronflantes ou de nouvelles étiquettes que l'on évoluera. Ni l'expression «dirty realism» ou «nouvelle architecture moraliste» (selon: «Architecture européenne depuis 1968») ne parviennent à décrire le patchwork européen. Et c'est tant mieux.

European style? An Italian is building in Paris for an international American company: IBM office building (Gino Valle)

Europäischer Stil? Ein Italiener baut in Paris für einen amerikanischen Weltkonzern: IBM-Bürogebäude (Gino Valle)

Un style européen? Un Italien construit à Paris pour une entreprise mondiale: immeuble de bureaux de la firme IBM (Gino Valle)

GÜNTER **BEHNISCH**
MARIO **BOTTA**
SANTIAGO **CALATRAVA**
NICHOLAS **GRIMSHAW**
GULLICHSEN, KAIRAMO &
VORMALA
ZAHA **HADID**
ADOLF **KRISCHANITZ**
IMRE **MAKOVECZ**
MECANOO
MIRALLES Y PINÓS
JEAN **NOUVEL**
PAOLO **PORTOGHESI**
SJOERD **SOETERS**

GÜNTER **BEHNISCH**

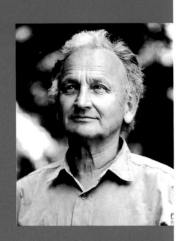

Günter Behnisch (* 1922 in Dresden) had already been working successfully as an architect for over thirty years (his major works were the tent roofs for the Munich Olympics, 1972) when in 1988 he was declared to be a Deconstructivist by the architectural critic, Charles Jencks. His design for the Hysolar Institute at Stuttgart University looked like a picture puzzle of a building which had been shaken by an earthquake or other natural disaster. Yet what seemed to fit so well into the Deconstructivist Zeitgeist was part of a logical development within Behnisch's design work: a playful, open style of building with modern light materials. The Olympia roof in Munich, the round school in Lorch (1973) and the Deutsches Postmuseum in Frankfurt (1990) are examples of an approach which leaves room for »surprises, incompleteness, and drollness« (Behnisch). His parliamentary building in Bonn (1992) is both a late work and his masterpiece.

Günter Behnisch (* 1922 in Dresden) hatte schon über dreißig Jahre erfolgreich als Architekt gearbeitet (sein Hauptwerk sind die Zeltdachkonstruktionen für die Olympiabauten in München, 1972), als 1988 der Engländer Charles Jencks Behnisch zum Dekonstruktivisten erklärte: Tatsächlich war sein Hysolar-Institut der Stuttgarter Universität zum Vexierbild einer durch Erdbeben oder andere Naturkatastrophen gebeutelten Baustruktur geraten. Doch das, was da sehr zeitgeistig dekonstruktivistisch wirkte, war nur die logische Fortsetzung bisheriger Entwurfsarbeit: eine spielerische, offene Bauweise aus modernen, leichten Materialien. Das Olympiadach von München, die heiter wirkende Schule von Lorch (1973) oder das Frankfurter Postmuseum (1990) sind Beispiele für eine Auffassung, die Raum für »Überraschendes, Unvollkommenes, Skurriles« (Behnisch) läßt. Sein Bundestag in Bonn (1992) ist Alterswerk und Meisterstück zugleich.

Günter Behnisch (* 1922 à Dresde) travaillait depuis trente ans avec succès comme architecte (œuvre principale: les toits de tente des pavillons olympiques à Munich, 1972) lorsqu'en 1988 Charles Jencks déclara que Behnisch était un déconstructiviste. En effet, son Institut Hysolar, à l'université de Stuttgart, ressemblait à un édifice endommagé par quelque tremblement de terre ou autre catastrophe naturelle. Mais ce qui paraissait très actuel, et dans la ligne du déconstructivisme, était en réalité la suite logique de ses réflexions: c'était une approche ludique, ouverte, avec des matériaux modernes, légers. Les toits des villages olympiques de Munich, l'école de Lorch (1973), ronde, joyeuse ou le Musée de la Poste de Francfort (1990) sont autant d'exemples d'une conception qui laisse la place «au surprenant, à l'inachevé, au comique» (Behnisch). Son Parlement fédéral (Bundestag, 1992), à Bonn, est à la fois œuvre de vieillesse et chef-d'œuvre.

Roof of German parliamentary building,
Bonn, seen from below: transparency and
technology are combined with consum-
mate ease

Deckenuntersicht im Deutschen Bundestag, Bonn: spielerische Mischung aus Transparenz und Technik

Vu de dessous, le plafond du Parlement allemand, Bonn: mélange tout en légèreté de
transparence et de technicité

LEYBOLD FACTORY ALZENAU (D) 1987

Corporate identity: »The quality of the work required in this engineering factory in Lower Franconia determines the architectural requirements« (Behnisch). This complicated building task called for production halls and laboratories, workshops and offices. It needed an architectonic »equivalent«, a memorable face. Behnisch gave it a number of faces, each appropriate to the specific task and function. The building has achieved international fame for its rounded projections picturesquely mirrored in a man-made lake. All in all, it is a complex which encourages »the relaxed co-operation of the whole workforce« (Behnisch).

Corporate Identity: »Der Anspruch an die Qualität der Arbeit dieser Maschinenfabrik in Unterfranken bestimmt den Architekturanspruch« (Behnisch). Eine komplizierte Bauaufgabe – Produktionshallen, Labor, Konstruktions- und Büroräume – suchte ihr architektonisches »Äquivalent«, ihr einprägsames Gesicht. Behnisch gab ihr gleich mehrere Gesichter, aber immer passend zur jeweiligen Aufgabe und Funktion. Inzwischen weltweit bekannt: abgerundete Kopfbauten, die sich pittoresk in einem vorgelagerten See spiegeln. Insgesamt eine Anlage, die zur »zwanglosen Zusammenarbeit aller Beschäftigten« (Behnisch) animiert.

Fierté d'un savoir-faire: «L'ambition de cette usine de machines d'effectuer un travail de qualité va de pair avec l'ambition architecturale» (Behnisch). Il s'agit d'un ouvrage complexe – hangars de production, laboratoires, bureaux et ateliers – qui cherchait sa «traduction» architecturale, son vrai visage. Behnisch lui en a donné plusieurs et chacun est adapté aux divers travaux et fonctions. Le monde entier connaît maintenant les coupoles de l'architecte qui, ici, se reflètent dans un lac. Le site dans son ensemble tend à créer une atmosphère de «détente pour les employés» (Behnisch).

The offices for the construction teams are located in the projections (below). Contrasting with this disciplined lay-out are the casual arrangements of glass and steel in the entrance area (remaining illustrations)

Die Gruppenbüros für die Konstruktion liegen in den Kopfbauten (unten); dieser disziplinierten Gestaltung stehen lockere Arrangements aus Glas und Stahl im Eingangsbereich gegenüber (übrige Abbildungen)

Les bureaux des équipes de construction sont situés dans les coupoles (en bas); face à cette configuration stricte, l'association plus fantaisiste de verre et d'acier de l'espace d'accueil (autres illustrations)

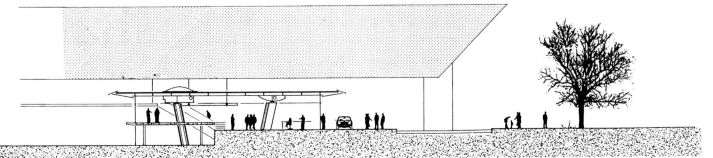

Above: The parliamentary building on the banks of the Rhine. Inside of the lobby (above right) an »angled« staircase connects the entrance portico (left page) with the assembly hall

Oben: Das Bundeshaus in den Rheinwiesen. In der Lobby (rechts oben) verbindet eine »schräge« Treppe das Eingangsbauwerk (linke Seite) mit dem Plenum

En haut: le bâtiment parlementaire au bord du Rhin. Dans le hall (en haut, à droite) un escalier oblique relie le bâtiment d'entrée (page de gauche) à la salle de session

GERMAN PARLIAMENTARY BUILDING BONN (D) 1992

The members of the German parliament wanted their new assembly area to be the architectural calling card of the Federal Republic of Germany, a young but firmly rooted democracy. This specification was taken literally by Behnisch & Partner. In their winning competition entry of 1973 they placed a circular assembly hall inside of a square glass block – a symbol of democracy and transparency. It is a building without any folkloric gestures or symbols of authority. It is an unpretentious building, even if the restaurant and lobby are unfortunately not entirely devoid of the agitated stylistic devices of the late 1980s.

Der neue Plenarbereich des deutschen Bundestages sollte nach Willen seiner Mitglieder zur gebauten Visitenkarte der Bundesrepublik Deutschland, einer zwar jungen, aber inzwischen fest im Volk verankerten Demokratie, werden. Behnisch & Partner haben diese Vorgabe in ihrem siegreichen Wettbewerbsbeitrag von 1973 sehr wörtlich genommen: Ein runder Plenarsaal steckt in einem Glasquader – Symbol für Demokratie und Transparenz. Ein Bauwerk ohne folkloristische Attitüden und ohne jegliches Autoritätsgehabe. Ein unprätentiöses Gebäude also, auch wenn Restaurant und Lobby sich leider der Stilmittel der aufgeregten End-80er-Jahre nicht ganz entziehen.

Les membres du Parlement allemand avaient souhaité que leur lieu d'assemblée fût un emblème de l'Allemagne fédérale, d'une démocratie jeune, certes, mais au ferme ancrage populaire. Behnisch & Partner, dans le projet qui leur valut la victoire au concours de 1973, ont pris les choses à la lettre: un espace circulaire s'inscrit dans un rectangle de verre – symbole de la démocratie et de la transparence. Pas de folklore, pour ce bâtiment, et pas d'affectation. Edifice sans prétention, donc, même si le restaurant et le hall d'accueil n'échappent pas aux tics stylistiques de la fin des années 80.

This is how the German parliament presents itself to the television audience. The »German Eagle« was designed by Behnisch (1992) to correspond with the circular assembly hall. Drawing: entrance (below), assembly area (centre), Rhine (top). Right: Art on the building I: blue wall ornamentation in the lobby

So präsentiert sich der Deutsche Bundestag auf der Fernsehmattscheibe: der »Bundesadler« (1992) nach einem Entwurf des Architekten Behnisch in Korrespondenz mit dem runden Plenum. Zeichnung: Eingang (unten), Plenarbereich (Mitte), Rhein (oben). Rechts: Kunst am Bau I: blauer Wandschmuck in der Lobby

C'est ainsi qu'apparaît le Parlement allemand sur le petit écran. «L'aigle fédéral» (1992) d'après un dessin de l'architecte Behnisch. Il est circulaire comme la salle elle-même. Dessin: entrée (en bas), salle de session (centre), le Rhin (en haut). A droite: l'art dans le bâtiment I: décoration murale bleue

Art on the Building II and III: The restaurant was decorated by the Italian painter, Nicola de Maria (above). Right: the so-called »presidential staircase« with banister. Designed by the architect, it is known as the »bird's nest«

Kunst am Bau II und III: Ausmalung des Restaurants durch den italienischen Maler Nicola de Maria (oben). Rechts: sogenannte »Präsidententreppe« mit Geländer, vom Architekten entworfen und »Vogelnest« genannt

L'art dans les bâtiments II et III: le restaurant a été décoré par le peintre italien Nicola de Maria (en haut). A droite: l'escalier dit «du président» et les balustrades, conçues par des architectes et dites «nid d'oiseau»

MARIO **BOTTA**

Architecture from the Ticino has a name: Mario Botta (* 1943 in Mendrisio). He used to be a representative of a regional approach. Working exclusively in the Ticino, he built almost only villas: the »fundamental constants in the history of human settlements, from primitive to modern architecture« (Botta). Today he is a cosmopolitan and builds in San Francisco and Tokyo. His houses oppose the rapacious development of the Ticino, but this is no longer Botta's only message. He now builds on a large scale, as with the cathedral at Evry (near Paris) or the Banca del Gottardo (Lugano). His architecture can be characterized as a »rule of three«: forceful geometries, façades which are usually chased and striped and inexorable determination to celebrate fantastic details. »Architecture must be a means of escape from the loss of identity, from the banality of everyday life, from the consumer society.«

Architektur aus dem Tessin hat einen Namen: Mario Botta (* 1943 in Mendrisio). Früher stand er für eine regionalistische Auffassung. Er baute ausschließlich im Tessin und vorwiegend Villen, die »fundamentalen Konstanten in der Geschichte der menschlichen Niederlassungen von der primitiven bis hin zur modernen Architektur« (Botta). Heute ist er Kosmopolit, steht zwischen San Francisco und Tokio. Außerdem sind seine Villen als Widerstand gegen die gedankenlose Zersiedlung im Tessin nicht mehr seine einzige Botschaft: Er baut Großes wie die Kathedrale von Evry (bei Paris) oder die Banca del Gottardo (Lugano). Seine Architektur läßt sich als »Dreisatz« charakterisieren: pralle Geometrien, eine ziselierte, meist streifenförmige Fassade und der unerbittliche Wille, phantastische Details zu zelebrieren. »Architektur muß ein Mittel sein, dem Verlust der Identität zu entgehen, der Banalisierung des Lebens, der Konsumgesellschaft.«

L'architecture du Tessin a un nom: Mario Botta (* 1943 à Mendrisio). Il fut d'abord le représentant d'une architecture régionaliste. Il travaillait exclusivement au Tessin et construisait surtout des villas, ces «constantes fondamentales dans l'histoire de l'habitat humain, depuis les temps primitifs jusqu'à ceux de l'architecture moderne» (Botta). Aujourd'hui, c'est un cosmopolite, il a un pied à San Francisco, l'autre à Tokyo, et ses villas tessinoises, construites en protestation contre l'urbanisation anarchique, ne sont plus son seul message. Il construit en grand, la cathédrale d'Evry, près de Paris ou la Banca del Gottardo, à Lugano, par exemple. On retrouve toujours trois éléments dans son style: des formes géométriques pleines, les façades ciselées et une volonté inébranlable de mettre en valeur des détails fantastiques. «L'architecture doit être un moyen d'échapper à la perte de l'identité, la banalisation de la vie, à la société de consommation.»

Insignia of Botta's architecture on the
Banca del Gottardo, Lugano: massive,
striped façades and bold, geometric forms

Insignien von Bottas Baukunst an der Banca del Gottardo, Lugano: Wuchtige Fassaden mit Streifenmuster, kühne geometri-
sche Formen der Baukörper

La Banca del Gottardo, à Lugano, porte la
marque de l'architecte Botta: façades mas-
sives au dessin en bandes, formes géométriques hardies des bâtiments

BANCA DEL GOTTARDO 1988
LUGANO (CH)

Mario Botta has succeeded here in unleashing on a large scale the mystical energy of his smaller, detached houses. The angular, crystalline buildings do not contain windows but rather slits and apertures. Inside, one has a vision of light and rain falling through these openings during a thunderstorm. A fortress of capitalism on the outside, on the inside it is a symphony of light and space whose poetry lets one forget that all of the activity here has to do with money.

Mario Botta ist es hier gelungen, die mystische Kraft seiner überschaubaren Einfamilienhäuser auch im größeren Maßstab zu entfesseln: Kantig und kristallin sind die Baukörper, die nicht durch Fenster, sondern durch Schlitze und Luken unterbrochen werden und die innen für die Vision sorgen, daß sich Licht wie Regen in einem Gewitter ins Haus stürzen; außen eine Trutzburg des Kapitals, innen eine Sinfonie aus Licht und Raum, die mittels Poesie vergessen läßt, daß man hier Geldgeschäfte tätigt.

Mario Botta a réussi ici à adapter à grande échelle la magie de ses petites maisons d'habitation: les bâtiments sont anguleux, nets comme le cristal et ne sont pas percés de fenêtres mais de meurtrières et de hublots qui, à l'intérieur, donnent l'impression que la lumière pénètre comme la pluie pendant un orage. De l'extérieur, château-fort du capital, de l'intérieur, symphonie de lumière et d'espace dont la poésie fait oublier que l'on traite ici des affaires d'argent.

Botta rejects the customary types of windows, indeed almost hates them. Instead, he makes openings in the wall at a few, small spots, as is traditional in southern Europe. Above: street front. Right page: towers at the back

Botta lehnt Fenster üblicher Art ab, haßt sie beinahe. Statt dessen durchbricht er die Wand nur an wenigen, winzigen Stellen, wie es im Süden Tradition ist. Oben: Straßenfront. Rechte Seite: Türme an der Rückseite

Botta refuse les fenêtres, quelles qu'elles soient, on peut presque dire qu'il les hait. Il préfère de rares et étroites failles dans le mur, comme c'est l'habitude dans le Sud. En haut: façade sur la rue. Page de droite: tours à l'arrière du bâtiment

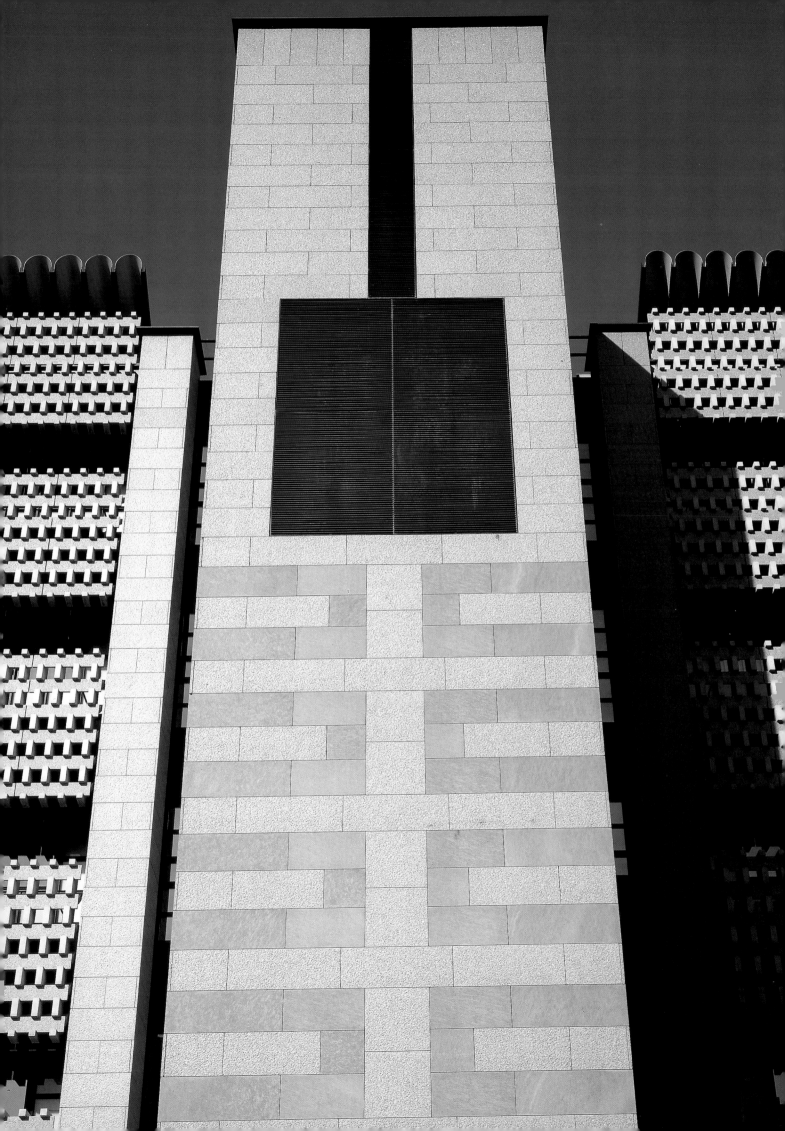

Unusual for a bank but typical for Botta:
walls, counters and desks are transformed
into striped sculptures (left page). Light and
space (above) add to the appeal. Sketches
by Botta: metamorphoses of a design

Bankunüblich, dafür typisch Botta: Wände,
Tresen und Pulte verwandeln sich zu Skulp-
turen im Streifenlook (linke Seite), Licht
und Raum (oben) verzaubern zusätzlich.
Skizzen von Botta: Metamorphosen eines
Entwurfes

Du rarement vu dans une banque, mais
typique de Botta: les murs, les comptoirs
et les guichets se transforment en sculptures formant un motif linéaire (page de
gauche). Lumière et espace (en haut) achè-
vent la transformation. Esquisses de Botta:
les métamorphoses d'un projet

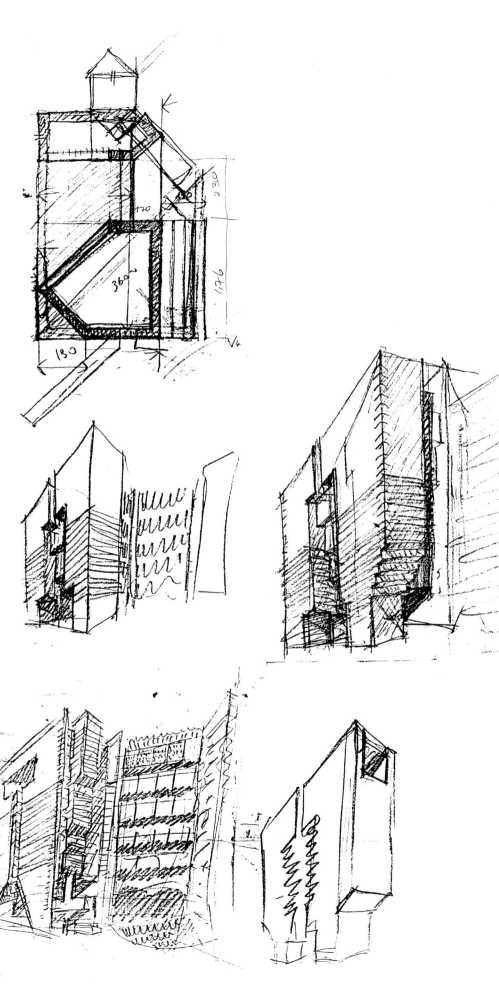

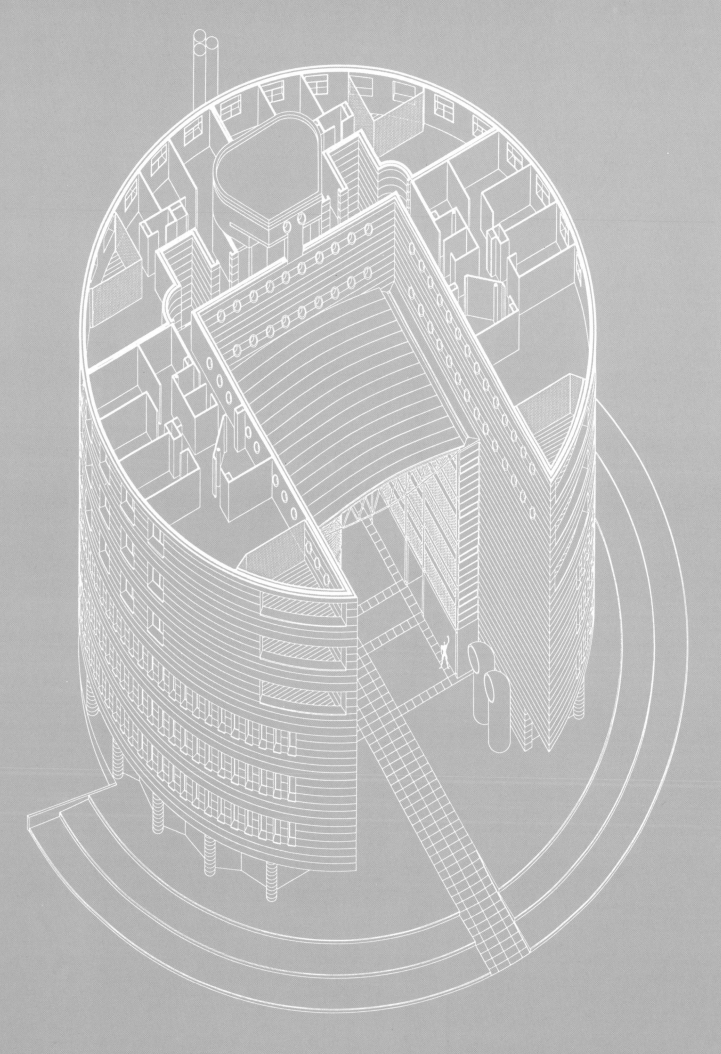

EDIFICIO RESIDENZIALE E COMMERCIALE A PARADISO, LUGANO   1986 - 1992

ASSONOMETRIA

COMMERCIAL AND RESIDENTIAL BUILDING 1991
LUGANO (CH)

Botta designed a symbolic building in his favoured cylindrical form for the Lugano suburb of Paradiso. He had already used this shape for his own office building in Lugano and for his Casa rotonda in Stabio (1982). In Paradiso, Botta cut open the cylinder on one side and emptied it, thereby creating an open atrium which he covered with glass. The remaining circular segments are each skilfully lit from two sides. The flexible plan means that the floors can be used in a variety of ways, for stores, banks, offices and apartments.

Für einen Standort im Luganer Seevorort Paradiso entwarf Botta ein zeichenhaftes Gebäude in der von ihm favorisierten Zylinderform. Diese hat er schon für sein eigenes Bürogebäude in Lugano und seine Casa rotonda in Stabio (1982) verwendet. Hier hat Botta den Zylinder an einer Seite aufgeschnitten und entkernt und den so entstandenen offenen Innenhof mit einem Glasdach geschlossen. Die verbliebenen Kreissegmente werden sehr geschickt jeweils von zwei Seiten belichtet. Der Grundrißzuschnitt ist flexibel, die Etagen können für Ladengeschäfte, Banken, Büros und Wohnungen genutzt werden.

Dans un site de bord de mer, à Paradiso, banlieue de Lugano, Botta a conçu un édifice pittoresque d'une forme qui lui est chère, le cylindre. Il a utilisé cette même forme pour son agence de Lugano et sa Casa rotonda de Stabio (1982). Ici, il a ouvert le cylindre sur un côté, l'a évidé et couvert la cour intérieure ainsi obtenue d'un toit de verre. Les autres segments du cercle peuvent, très habilement, être chacun éclairé de deux côtés. La répartition des espaces est si souple que, selon les étages l'immeuble abrite des magasins, des banques, des bureaux et des appartements.

Left page: The axonometry shows how apartments were placed around the rectangular atrium in the upper storey. On the outside the building is of stone (Botta's preference) and on the inside of filigreed glass and steel (top). The stairwell is in the glass barrel (above)

Linke Seite: Die Axonometrie zeigt, wie im oberen Geschoß um den rechtwinkligen Innenhof Wohnungen gelegt wurden. Außen steinern (wie Botta es bevorzugt), innen filigran aus Stahl und Glas (ganz oben). In der gläsernen Tonne (oben) befindet sich das Treppenhaus

Page de gauche: l'axonométrie montre comment des appartements ont été disposés en bordure de la cour intérieure, rectangulaire. Pierre à l'extérieur (selon la préférence de l'architecte), verre et acier en filigrane à l'intérieur (tout en haut). L'escalier (en haut) est logé dans un cylindre de verre

DARO HOUSE 1992
DARO (CH)

This detached house rises up against
the stony landscape of the Ticino and
does not make the slightest overtures
to either the landscape or the neighbouring buildings. Instead, it has cut itself off, like Noah's Ark, from unwel-
come visitors. The link to the outside
world is provided by narrow openings
in the wall and by an atrium. This time
Botta chose the striking form of the
truncated hull of a ship: the bow is
wedged in the hillside and the stern
points towards the landscape. Here is
an ark which has come to rest.

Schroff erhebt sich die Villa aus der
steinigen Landschaft des Tessins; sie
versucht nicht im geringsten, auf Landschaft oder Nachbarbebauung einzugehen. Statt dessen schottet sie sich ab,
wie Noahs Arche, vor unerwünschten
Besuchern. Die Verbindung nach außen wird nur durch schmale Maueröff-
nungen und ein nach innen gelegtes
Atrium hergestellt. Als markante Groß-
form hat Botta diesmal einen abge-
schnittenen Schiffskörper ausgewählt:
Der Bug steckt im Hang, und das
Heck weist in die Landschaft – eine Arche, die ihre endgültige Position gefunden hat.

Cette maison d'habitation surgit dans
le paysage pierreux du Tessin sans
chercher le moins du monde à se ma-
rier avec le cadre naturel ou l'habitat
voisin. Plutôt, insubmersible comme
l'arche de Noé, elle semble se proté-
ger de visiteurs indésirables. Le lien
avec l'extérieur ne se fait que par
d'étroites ouvertures dans les murs et
une cour intérieure. La forme prédomi-
nante est cette fois une carène de bateau: la proue vient donner contre la
colline et la poupe s'élève dans le paysage – l'arche a trouvé sa place.

Drawing: the »ark« and the hillside. A loggia has been pushed into the central living area and supplies it with light from three sides (above). As indicated by the white walls and filigreed banisters, Botta's style of fashioning interiors is so conclusive that additional furnishings become almost impossible – as almost all of his private clients have been forced to acknowledge

Zeichnung: Die »Arche« und der Berghang. Eine Loggia ist in den zentralen Wohnraum geschoben worden und gibt ihm Licht von drei Seiten (oben). Mit weißen Wänden und filigranem Geländerwerk gestaltet Botta so zwingend, daß die Möblierung beinahe unmöglich wird – eine Erfahrung, die fast alle seine privaten Bauherren machen

Dessin: l'«arche» et la colline. Dans la pièce d'habitation centrale, on a intégré une loggia qui donne de la lumière par trois côtés (en haut). Avec ses murs blancs et ses balustrades filiformes, Botta crée une ambiance si forte qu'il est presque impossible d'y ajouter des meubles – presque tous ses clients ont fait cette expérience

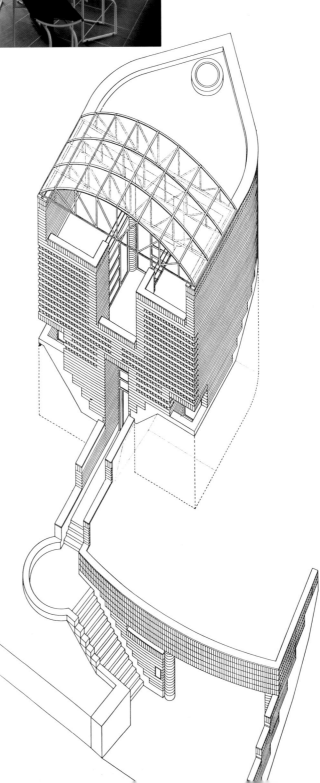

SANTIAGO CALATRAVA

His thirst for knowledge seems unquenchable. Santiago Calatrava Valls (* 1951 in Valencia) attended art school and studied architecture. This was followed by a further degree – in urban studies – and by a full course in civil engineering, in which he obtained a doctorate. Calatrava is an exception in Europe, and cannot be placed into a category. Is he a tradition-conscious but playful Spaniard or, because he set up his office in Zurich in 1981, more of a predictable »northern Swiss«? In any event, he is a man who forges links between north and south, between sculpture and construction – and he builds bridges, such as the Puente Bach de Roda in Barcelona (1987). Over 140 meters long and strung like a harp, it is a symbol of engineering art. The builder of bridges (for Mérida, Seville, Bordeaux) became an architect of train stations (Lucerne, Zurich, Berlin-Spandau). With designs for the cathedral of St. John the Divine in New York and for the Reichstag in Berlin he is reaching for new dimensions.

Sein Wissensdurst scheint unstillbar zu sein: Santiago Calatrava Valls (* 1951 in Valencia) besuchte die Kunstschule und studierte Architektur. Dann folgten Nachdiplom in Urbanistik und ein komplettes Bauingenieurstudium mit abschließender Promotion. Calatrava bildet eine Ausnahme in Europa; einzuordnen ist er nicht: Vielleicht traditionsbewußter, aber verspielter Spanier oder doch eher kalkulierbarer »Nordschweizer«, weil er in Zürich 1981 ein Büro gegründet hat? In jedem Fall ist er ein Mann, der Brücken schlägt zwischen Norden und Süden, zwischen Skulptur und Konstruktion – und einer, der Brücken baut: Die Bach-de-Roda-Brücke in Barcelona (1987) ist gespannt wie eine Harfe und über 140 Meter lang: zeichenhafte Ingenieurkunst. Aus dem Brückenbauer (für Mérida, Sevilla, Bordeaux) wurde der Bahnhofsarchitekt (Luzern, Zürich, Berlin-Spandau). Mit Entwürfen für die Kathedrale St. John the Divine in New York und den Reichstag in Berlin greift er nach neuen Dimensionen.

Sa soif d'apprendre semble inextinguible. Santiago Calatrava Valls (* 1951 à Valence) fit des études d'architecte. Ensuite il y ajouta un diplôme d'urbanisme et tout un cursus d'ingénieur en bâtiment: Calatrava représente une exception en Europe. Il n'est pas classifiable: est-ce un Espagnol, traditionnaliste mais fantaisiste ou bien un Suisse raisonnable, depuis qu'il a, en 1981, fondé une agence à Zurich? C'est, en tout cas, un homme qui jette des ponts entre le Nord et le Sud, entre la sculpture et la construction – et c'est un homme qui construit des ponts, le Puente Bach de Roda, à Barcelone, 1987, par exemple. Il est tendu comme une harpe et mesure plus de 140 mètres de long – une prouesse d'ingénieur, un dessin d'architecte. Le constructeur de ponts (à Mérida, Séville, Bordeaux) se fit architcte de gares (Lucerne, Zurich, Berlin-Spandau). Avec des projets pour la cathédrale St John the Divine, à New York et pour le Reichstag de Berlin, il atteint à une dimension nouvelle.

Steel architecture on anatomical models,
Stadelhofen city railway station, Zurich

Stahlbaukunst am Zürcher S-Bahnhof Stadelhofen nach anatomischen Vorbildern

Exercice de construction en acier à la gare
Stadelhofen de Zurich, inspiré de modèles
anatomiques

ALAMILLO BRIDGE SEVILLE (E) 1992

It was through his bridges that Calatrava became really famous and he once compared their construction to the composition of a Mozart symphony. When the solo instrument in »Symphonica Concertante« begins to play, it has the same surprising effect as the arches of Calatrava's bridges, for they also seem to appear out of nowhere. This is the southernmost bridge on the Guadalquivir and was built for the Seville Expo. Its sloping pylon gives it a particular force and its resemblance to a harp or a lyre is certainly not accidental.

Den Bau von Brücken, die Calatrava erst richtig berühmt machten, hat der Architekt einmal mit der Komposition einer Mozartsinfonie verglichen. So wie in der »Symphonica Concertante« das Soloinstrument einsetzt, genauso überraschend tauchen auch Calatravas Brückenbögen aus dem Nichts auf. Die südlichste Brücke über den Guadalquivir, die im Rahmen der Weltausstellung in Sevilla gebaut wurde, betont Calatrava mit einem schräggestellten Pylon: Das Bild einer in den Boden gerammten Harfe oder Lyra entstand – und war sicher kein Zufall.

Calatrava a un jour comparé la construction de ponts, qui l'a révélé au public, à la composition d'une symphonie mozartienne. Comme intervient l'instrument soliste dans la «Symphonica concertante», ainsi apparaissent, brusquement, comme du néant, les arches des ponts de Calatrava. Le pont qui enjambe, au sud, le Guadalquivir, construit dans le cadre de l'exposition universelle de Séville, a été souligné par un pylone penché: cela donne naissance à l'image d'une harpe ou d'une lyre plantée dans le sol, ce qui n'est sûrement pas un hasard.

REICHSTAG (PROJECT) BERLIN (D) 1993

Calatrava's prize-winning design for the extension to the Berlin Reichstag is highly controversial. At first glance the new dome appears too large and recalls a gigantic Easter egg. The assembly hall is located deep within the interior; in a manner of speaking, it has been lowered into the cellar. Nevertheless, Calatrava's sketches and ideas show that he took a very careful and sensitive approach to the old building. He wanted to do justice to it in his own way, which could be expressed in the maxim, »We must always seek a path where truth does not suffer and emotion does not hunger« (Bruno Taut).

Der preisgekrönte Entwurf Calatravas für den Ausbau des Berliner Reichstages ist heftig umstritten. Die neue Kuppel wirkt auf den ersten Blick zu groß und erinnert an ein gigantisches Osterei. Der Plenarsaal ist tief ins Innere, sozusagen in den »Keller«, versenkt. Trotzdem: Calatravas Skizzen und Ideen weisen nach, daß der Architekt sich sehr langsam und sensibel dem Altbau genähert hat. Er wollte ihm auf seine eigene Weise gerecht werden, nach dem Motto: »Wir müssen ständig den Weg suchen, bei dem die Wahrheit nicht leidet und das Gefühl nicht hungert« (Bruno Taut).

Le projet de Calatrava pour la réfection du Reichstag à Berlin, qui lui a valu un prix, est violemment contesté. Au premier abord, la nouvelle coupole semble trop grande et fait penser à un énorme œuf de Pâques. La salle de session est située en profondeur, comme «en sous-sol». Et pourtant: on comprend aux esquisses qu'il a approché l'ancien bâtiment au plus près, et avec beaucoup de sensibilité. A sa façon, il voulait lui rendre hommage, dans le sens où Bruno Taut dit: «Nous devons sans cesse chercher le chemin par lequel la vérité ne souffre pas et le sentiment ne dépérit pas».

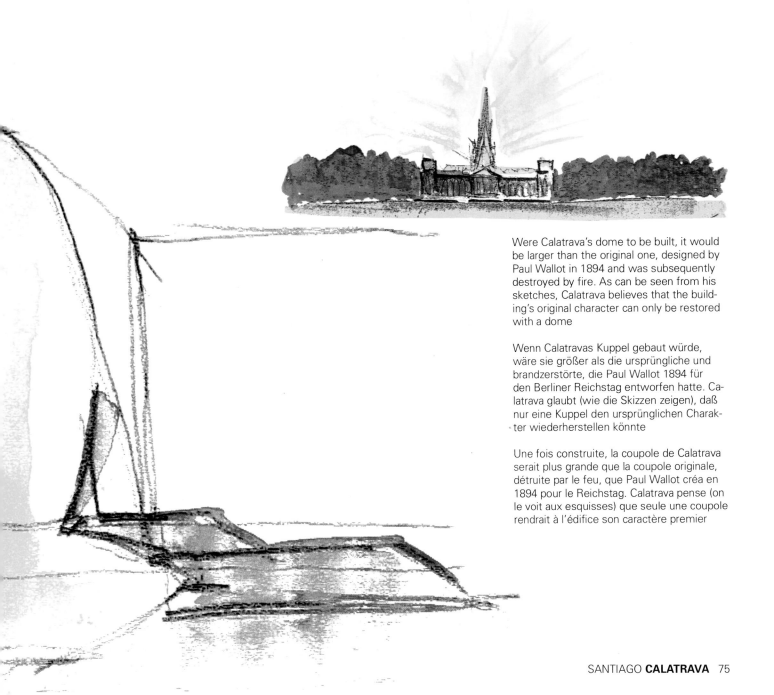

Were Calatrava's dome to be built, it would be larger than the original one, designed by Paul Wallot in 1894 and was subsequently destroyed by fire. As can be seen from his sketches, Calatrava believes that the building's original character can only be restored with a dome

Wenn Calatravas Kuppel gebaut würde, wäre sie größer als die ursprüngliche und brandzerstörte, die Paul Wallot 1894 für den Berliner Reichstag entworfen hatte. Calatrava glaubt (wie die Skizzen zeigen), daß nur eine Kuppel den ursprünglichen Charakter wiederherstellen könnte

Une fois construite, la coupole de Calatrava serait plus grande que la coupole originale, détruite par le feu, que Paul Wallot créa en 1894 pour le Reichstag. Calatrava pense (on le voit aux esquisses) que seule une coupole rendrait à l'édifice son caractère premier

STADELHOFEN STATION ZURICH (CH) 1990

»Along with steel, concrete is the material of this century« (Calatrava). Calatrava used both materials for the city railway station at Stadelhofen, in the centre of Zurich. The station's subterranean base looks as if it has been carved out of stone – a cave for public transport. It is appropriate to Zurich's mountainous surroundings, but has actually been created out of prefabricated elements. Underground, one is reminded of a mammoth's brawny bone structure, but up on the platform the steel profiles resemble the elegant skeleton of a fish.

»Beton ist zusammen mit Stahl das Material des Jahrhunderts« (Calatrava). Für die S-Bahnstation Stadelhofen mitten in Zürich hat Calatrava beide Stoffe verwendet. Die unterirdische Basis des Bahnhofs wirkt wie aus Stein gehauen – eine Höhle für den Nahverkehr. Sie paßt zur gebirgigen Umgebung Zürichs – aber sie besteht in Wirklichkeit aus vorgefertigten Elementen. Mag man dort unten eher an den bulligen Knochenbau eines Mammuts erinnert werden – oben auf dem Bahnsteig könnten die Stahlprofile der Eleganz eines Fischskeletts abgeschaut sein.

«Le béton est, avec l'acier, le matériau du siècle» (Calatrava). Pour cette gare située en pleine ville, il a utilisé les deux. La base de la gare, souterraine, semble taillée dans la masse – une grotte pour trains de banlieue. Elle se marie à l'environnement montagneux de la ville, et pourtant elle est composée d'éléments préfabriqués. Si, en bas, on pense à l'ossature massive d'un mammouth, en haut, sur le quai, les fines poutrelles d'acier ont l'élégance d'un squelette de poisson.

Zurich has a city railway line between the mountain and the lake. Stadelhofen station has been dug into it (left page: basement, below: platform area)

Zwischen Zürichberg und -see verläuft eine S-Bahn-Trasse. Darin eingegraben ist der Bahnhof Stadelhofen (linke Seite: Basement, unten: Bahnsteigbereich)

A Zurich, entre lac et montagne, une voie ferroviaire. Une gare y a été creusée, la gare de Stadelhofen (page de gauche: sous-sol, en bas: quai des voyageurs)

Strong and brawny like the bones of a
mammoth: the artificial »mountains« which
form the base of Stadelhofen station

Kräftig und bullig wie Mammutknochen:
das künstliche »Gebirge«, das die Basis
zum S-Bahnhof Stadelhofen bildet

Solide et massive comme des os de mammouth, la «montagne» artificielle qui forme
la base de la gare Stadelhofen

NICHOLAS **GRIMSHAW**

For a long time, he stood in the shadow of the great tsars of British High Tech, Norman Foster and Richard Rogers. Nicholas Grimshaw (* 1939 in London) has now come so far, however, that he designed Great Britain's pavilion at the recent World Exposition. At the latest since Expo 1992 and his »cathedral of water«, Grimshaw can be counted amongst the leading lights of the English version of the so-called High Tech style. »Our buildings are unusually economical and reflect the absolute necessity of conserving energy and saving resources«, says Grimshaw, and he is justified in pointing out that the significance of his buildings does not lie solely in their outer, gleaming, metal cladding. The powerful waterfall of his Seville pavilion for example, only used a quarter of the energy that would normally be required. Grimshaw's most important works are commercial buildings, such as the printing works for the Financial Times in London's Docklands (1988).

Er stand immer ein wenig im Schatten der großen britischen High-Tech-Zaren Norman Foster und Richard Rogers. Doch jetzt hat es Nicholas Grimshaw (* 1939 in London) so weit gebracht, Großbritannien baulich auf einer Weltausstellung zu repräsentieren. Spätestens seit der Expo 1992 und seiner »Kathedrale des Wassers« gehört Grimshaw zu den Lichtgestalten des sogenannten High-Tech-Stils englischer Prägung. »Unsere Gebäude sind ungewöhnlich ökonomisch und reflektieren, daß es unbedingt notwendig ist, Energie zu sparen und Ressourcen zu schonen«, sagt er und weist zu Recht darauf hin, daß es nicht allein auf die vordergründigen glitzernden Metallkleider seiner Häuser ankommt. Die gewaltige Wasserkaskade seines Sevilla-Pavillons spart zum Beispiel ein Viertel der normalerweise notwendigen Energie. Grimshaws wichtigste Bauten sind Gewerbebauten, wie das Druckereigebäude der Financial Times in den Londoner Docklands (1988).

Il fut toujours un peu dans l'ombre des stars du High Tech britannique, Norman Foster et Richard Rogers. Mais à présent, Nicholas Grimshaw (* 1939 à Londres) en est arrivé à représenter son pays lors d'une exposition universelle. Depuis l'Exposition de 1992 et sa Cathédrale de l'eau, Grimshaw fait partie des tout grands de ce que l'on appelle le style High Tech, version anglaise. «Nos constructions sont particulièrement économiques et montrent qu'il est indispensable de modérer nos dépenses d'énergie et de respecter les ressources», dit-il en faisant remarquer que ce qui est important dans ses bâtiments n'est pas seulement leur revêtement de métal brillant. A titre d'exemple: l'énorme cascade de son pavillon de Séville permet d'économiser un quart de l'énergie nécessaire. Les constructions les plus importantes de Grimshaw sont des bâtiments industriels, comme l'imprimerie du Financial Times, dans le quartier des docks, à Londres (1988).

Joint in interior. Element of the façade of
the British Pavilion, Seville Expo

Innenliegender Knotenpunkt, Fassadenkon-
struktion des britischen Pavillons, Expo
Sevilla

A l'intérieur: faisceau: élément de structure
de la façade du pavillon britannique à l'Expo
de Séville

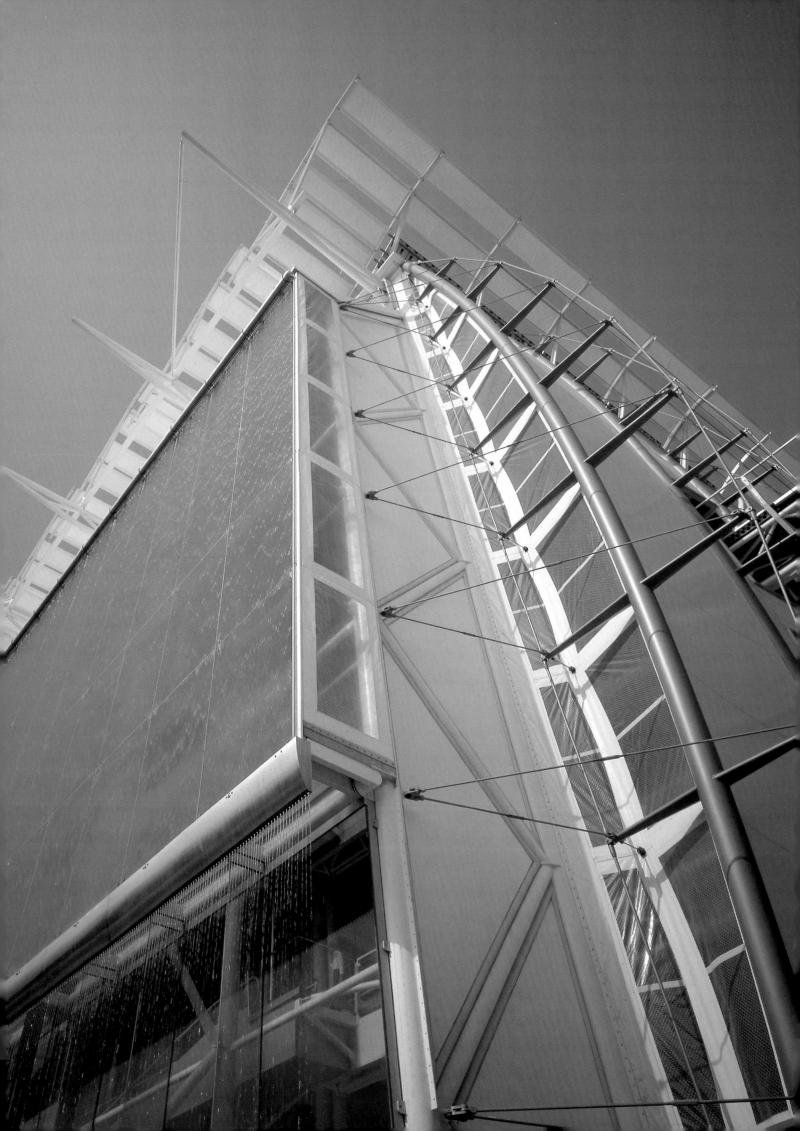

BRITISH PAVILION 1992
SEVILLE (E)

Apart from the fact that the escalators lie inside of the building, Grimshaw's British Pavilion at the Seville Expo copies the Centre Pompidou in Paris. Nevertheless, the »box with the waterfall« and the roof sails of integrated solar cells was amongst the most exciting national pavilions. Grimshaw demonstrated that the coupling of High Tech yearnings and ecological responsibility could have an exciting appearance. At a second glance, the pavilion is more refined – particularly in its details – than the martial Centre Pompidou. It is also an energy-saver.

Grimshaws Pavillon auf der Expo in Sevilla kopiert das Pariser Centre Pompidou, einmal abgesehen davon, daß die Rolltreppen hier innen liegen. Trotzdem gehörte die »Kiste mit dem Wasserfall« und den Dachsegeln mit integrierten Solarzellen zu den aufregendsten Nationalpavillons der Ausstellung. Bewies doch Grimshaw, daß die Paarung aus High-Tech-Sehnsucht und ökologischer Vernunft ein aufregendes Gesicht haben kann, denn auf den zweiten Blick ist der Pavillon besonders im Detail feiner als das martialische Centre Pompidou – und ein Energiesparer dazu.

Le pavillon britannique de l'Expo de Séville est copié sur le Centre Pompidou, à Paris, à cette nuance près que l'escalier mécanique est ici à l'intérieur. Pourtant, la «caisse à la cascade» avec son toit de voiles de bateau aux cellules solaires intégrées fut l'un des pavillons les plus enthousiasmants de la manifestation. Grimshaw y fait la preuve que l'association de réminiscences High Tech et de bon sens écologique peut produire un effet intéressant. En effet, en y regardant de plus près, le Pavillon apparaît plus subtil dans les détails, que le martial édifice parisien – et, de plus, il est écologique.

300 000 litres of water were kept in motion to cool the front façade (above). The sketch explains how the outside temperature is thereby reduced by approximately 20 degrees Fahrenheit in the interior.

300 000 Liter Wasser waren ständig in Bewegung, um die Fassade zu kühlen (oben); die Skizze erläutert die Folgen davon: Reduktion der Außentemperatur um etwa 11° C im Innern.

300 000 litres d'eau étaient continuellement en mouvement pour refroidir la façade (en haut); l'esquisse en montre le résultat: il faisait à l'intérieur environ 20 degrés Fahrenheit de moins qu'à l'extérieur.

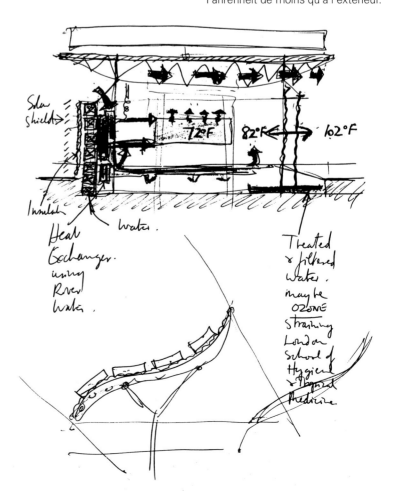

The exterior walls (above left and drawing) consist of a multi-layered climatic skin. The interior design reflects the image that the industrial nations in Seville had selected for themselves: futuristic, technoid, perfect

Die Seitenwände (links oben und Zeichnung) bestehen aus einer mehrschichtigen Klimahaut. Die Innenarchitektur entspricht dem Image, das sich die Industrienationen in Sevilla gern zulegen wollten: futuristisch, technoid, perfekt

Les murs latéraux (en haut à gauche et dessin) sont constitués d'un matériau isolant multi-couches. L'architecture intérieure correspond à l'image que les nations industrialisées souhaitaient donner d'elles-mêmes: elle est futuriste, technicisée, perfectionniste

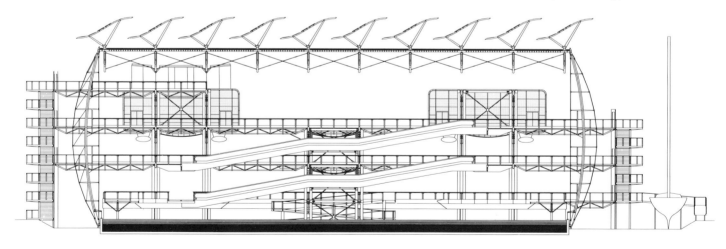

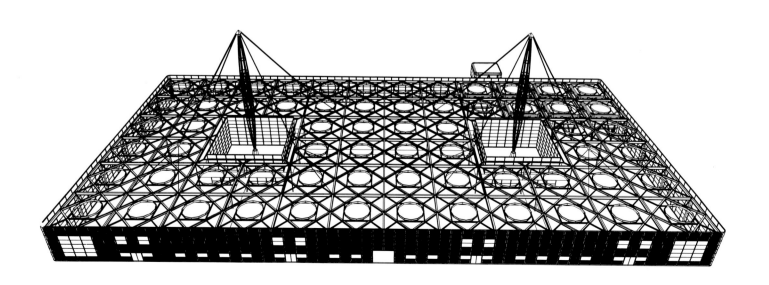

IGUS FACTORY AND HEADQUARTERS 1993
COLOGNE (D)

Grimshaw's strength is industrial architecture and is reflected in his objectives: the honest box, in which industrial products are manufactured, and whose purpose is communicated to the outside world via architecture. As with the Vitra factory in Weil am Rhein or the Financial Times Building in London, Grimshaw also succeeded in Cologne in slightly »exaggerating« his very harmless façades, which are a faithful product of prefabricated, i. e. industrial, architecture. Here, parts of the roof structure have been hung onto two, banana-shaped trussed pylons.

Grimshaws Stärke ist getreu seiner eigenen Zielsetzungen die Industriearchitektur: die ehrliche Box, in der industrielle Waren gefertigt werden und bei der sich dies via Architektur nach außen mitteilt. Wie bei Vitra in Weil am Rhein oder dem Financial Times Building in London gelingt es Grimshaw auch in Köln, seine sehr harmlosen Fassaden, die ein treues Abbild vorgefertigter, also industrieller Bauweise sind, ein wenig zu »überhöhen«. Hier sind es zwei bananenförmige Fachwerkpylone, an denen Teile der Dachkonstruktion aufgehängt sind.

Fidèle aux buts qu'il s'est fixés, Grimshaw excelle dans la construction industrielle: boîtes sans artifices dans lesquelles sont fabriquées des marchandises et qui interpellent le monde extérieur par le biais de l'architecture. Comme pour l'usine Vitra, à Weil am Rhein, ou le Financial Times Building à Londres, Grimshaw réussit à Cologne à «animer» un peu une façade très neutre, produit typique de la construction préfabriquée. Ici, ce sont deux pylônes en forme de bananes auxquels sont fixés des éléments du bâtiment.

Metal crate with supports. Despite rational prefabrication (above, right), an impressive façade was created. Drawing: the perspective explains the composition of the roof structure

Blechkiste mit Halterung: Trotz rationeller Vorfertigung (oben, rechts) entstand eine beeindruckende Fassade. Zeichnung: Die Perspektive erklärt den Aufbau der Dachkonstruktion

Caisse métallique et système d'attache: malgré le côté préfabriqué (en haut, à droite), la façade est réussie. Dessin: la perspective explicite le procédé de construction du toit

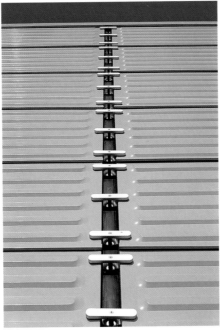

High Tech at its best. Unclad steel and iron
– an appropriate outfit for a workshop or
production hall

High-Tech »at its best«, Stahl und Blech, un-
verkleidet – ein Outfit, das zu einer Werk-
statt oder Fertigungshalle paßt

High Tech «at its best», acier et métal sans
fioriture – une installation qui convient bien
à un atelier

WESTERN MORNING NEWS 1993
PLYMOUTH (GB)

The building acknowledges its vicinity
to the coast. In neither its details nor
in its overall appearance does this
»newspaper ship« for the printing
works of the »Western Morning
News« deny what it was modelled on.
The control room rises up over the
glass-contained printing works in the
form of a ship's bridge. The walls
could have been designed by sail-
makers and (once again) stern and
bow can be clearly made out. And
Grimshaw has again magically transformed dry technology with a trace of
poetry.

Das Haus zollt der Küstennähe
Respekt: Das Zeitungsschiff der
»Western Morning News« verleugnet
seine Vorbilder weder im Detail noch
beim Gesamtauftritt: Über der gläsernen Druckerei thront die Kommando-
zentrale in Form einer Schiffsbrücke.
Die Wände könnten von Segelma-
chern entworfen sein; Heck und Bug
sind (wieder einmal) deutlich auszuma-
chen. Und Grimshaw ist es erneut gelungen, spröde Technik mit einer Spur
Poesie zu verzaubern.

L'immeuble s'inspire du paysage mari-
time: le bateau-journal ne renie ses
modèles ni dans le détail ni dans
l'aspect général. Au-dessus de l'imprimerie, toute en verre, la passerelle de
commandement. Les murs auraient
pu être conçus par des fabricants de
voiles, proue et poupe sont (encore
une fois) facilement reconnaissables.
Et, une fois de plus, Grimshaw est par-
venu à poétiser l'aride technique.

The printing works as a ship (above), whose walls have been delicately and accurately streched over it (left page). As in the belly of a ship, the enormous rotary printing machines disappear into the interior

Die Druckerei als Schiff (oben), deren Wände diffizil und präzise abgespannt werden (linke Seite). Wie in einem Schiffsbauch verschwinden hier die riesigen Rotationsdruckmaschinen im Innern

Un bateau-imprimerie (en haut), dont les murs sont montés grâce à une technique délicate et précise (page de gauche). Les gigantesques rotatives se trouvent ici en profondeur, comme dans le ventre d'un bateau

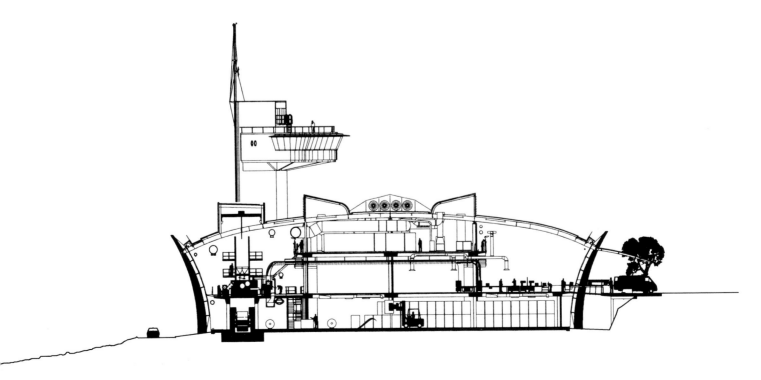

GULLICHSEN, KAIRAMO & VORMALA

Perhaps it is Finland's climate and its distance from European cities which has allowed the modern architecture of the 1920s and 1930s to be preserved here in a virtually unadulterated form and also facilitated its further, restrained development. The office of Kristian Gullichsen (* 1932), Erkki Kairamo (* 1936) and Timo Vormala (* 1942) is the most important executor of this legacy. Indeed, Gullichsen was trained under the father of modern Finnish architecture, Alvar Aalto. When one looks at their housing projects (e.g. Kairamo's semi-detached houses in Espoo, 1990), even the practiced observer is shaken: filigreed iron and glass, area and space, as if it were a piece by De Stijl. All three architects are concerned with »variations on Modernism«, but this has different meanings for each of them. In the best tradition of Le Corbusier, Gullichsen is concerned not only with bold glass and steel creations but also with the composition of walls and the way that light is used in space.

Es mögen Klima und die Ferne von den europäischen Metropolen sein: In Finnland hat sich die moderne Architektur aus den 20er und 30er Jahren nahezu in Reinkultur erhalten und sanft weiterentwickelt. Dem Büro von Kristian Gullichsen (* 1932), Erkki Kairamo (* 1936) und Timo Vormala (* 1942) kommt dabei die Rolle des wichtigsten Erbverwalters zu. Schließlich hat Gullichsen beim Vater der modernen finnischen Architektur, Alvar Aalto, gelernt. Ihre Wohnhausprojekte (z. B. Doppelhaus in Espoo von Kairamo, 1990) lassen den geübten Betrachter erschauern: filigranes Eisen und Glas, Fläche und Raum, als wär's ein Stück von De Stijl. Die drei Chefs des Büros haben »Variationen der Moderne« zum Thema, aber eben unterschiedliche. Bei Gullichsen bedeutet dies in bester Tradition eines Le Corbusier nicht nur kühne Glas-Stahl-Kreationen, sondern auch Kompositionen aus Wand und Raum im inszenierten Licht.

Peut-être est-ce le climat et l'éloignement des métropoles européennes: en Finlande, l'architecture moderne des années 20 et 30 se retrouve presque à l'état pur, n'ayant subi qu'une faible évolution. Aussi l'agence de Kristian Gullichsen (* 1932), Erkki Kairamo (* 1936) et Timo Vormala (* 1942) en est-elle la principale héritière. D'ailleurs, Gullichsen a appris son métier avec Alvar Aalto, le père de l'architecture moderne finlandaise. En feuilletant leurs projets de maisons (par exemple, maison double à Espoo par Kairamo, 1990), l'amateur d'architecture n'en revient pas: métal en filigrane et verre, surfaces, espaces, on est en plein De Stijl. Les trois chefs font des variations sur le thème moderne, mais des variations différentes. Chez Gullichsen, dans la meilleure tradition de Le Corbusier, ce ne sont pas seulement d'audacieuses structures de verre et d'acier mais aussi une répartition des espaces dans une mise en scène de lumière.

Carrying on in the tradition of the Bauhaus:
the detail solutions in the semi-detached
house in Espoo, Helsinki

Der Tradition des Bauhauses verpflichtet:
Detaillösungen im Doppelhaus in Espoo bei
Helsinki

Fidélité au Bauhaus oblige: détails de la maison jumelée de Espoo près d'Helsinki

STOCKMANN DEPARTMENT STORE EXTENSION 1989
HELSINKI (SF)

The Stockmann department store lies in the heart of Helsinki, surrounded by buildings by the Finnish heroes, Eero and Eliel Saarinen and Alvar Aalto. Although the massive original building (1930) with its stepped top storeys (architect: Sigurd Frosterus) was formally lengthened, the expressive brick façade was also given a crystalline, glass extension. It was more difficult to link the new with the old on the other side of the store, where the new building meets up with a former office building in a Neo-Renaissance style.

Das Kaufhaus Stockmann liegt im Herzen Helsinkis und inmitten von Bauten der finnischen Heroen Eero und Eliel Saarinen sowie Alvar Aalto. Der gewaltige Kaufhausaltbau von 1930 mit seinen abgetreppten Dachgeschossen (Architekt: Sigurd Frosterus) wird formal verlängert. Doch erhält die expressive Backsteinfassade ein gläsernkristallines Pendant. Schwieriger war der Anschluß auf der anderen Kaufhausseite. Dort stößt ein früheres Geschäftshaus im Stil der Neorenaissance an den Neubau.

Le grand magasin Stockmann se trouve au cœur d'Helsinki, parmi des constructions des célèbres architectes finlandais Eero et Eliel Saarinen et Alvar Aalto. On a agrandi le massif immeuble de 1930, avec ses derniers étages en terrasses (architecte: Sigurd Frosterus) et donné à l'expressive façade de brique un pendant de verre cristallin. De l'autre côté du magasin, la connection a été plus difficile. Le nouvel édifice se trouve accolé à un ancien magasin de style néo-renaissance.

The architects used a visual caesura as well as a tower to create a transition to the original turn-of-the-century building (above left). The tower is reminiscent of El Lissitzky's Lenin Tribune Tower. An emphatic modernity distinguishes the new building (right page) and there is also a dynamic new interpretation on the old theme of department store and air well (above right)

Die Architekten lösen den Übergang zum Altbau aus der Jahrhundertwende (oben links) durch optische Zäsur und einen Turm: Reminiszenz an El Lissitzkys Lenin Tribune Tower. Pralle Modernität für den Neubauabschnitt (rechte Seite) und die dynamische Neuinterpretation des alten Themas Warenhaus-Lichthof (oben rechts)

Pour relier la nouvelle construction à l'ancienne (en haut, à gauche), les architectes ont choisi de construire une tour et de pratiquer une césure optique: on pense à la Lenin Tribune Tower de El Lissitzky. Modernité éclatante pour la partie nouvelle (page de droite) et réinterprétation dynamique du thème ancien des magasins (en haut, a gauche)

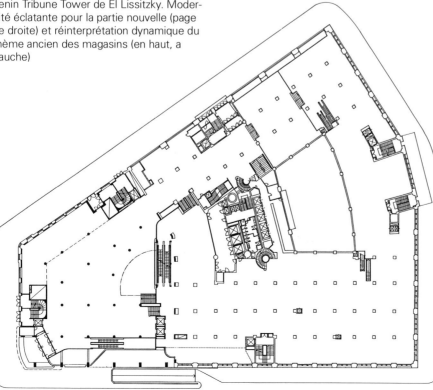

SEMI-DETACHED HOUSE 1990
ESPOO (SF)

Erkki Kairamo always builds the same type of cubic house – far from any clicheés to do with luxury. This semi-detached house in Helsinki's western suburb of Espoo looks like having gone astray from the Riviera. Nevertheless, it has been carefully prepared for Finland's icy winter weather. The windows' filigreed mullions are actually ensconced in triple-glazing. On the southern side a system of terraces, balconies and garages has been placed as a buffer zone against the cold.

Erkki Kairamo baut – fern von jedem Luxusklischee – immer den gleichen, kubischen Villentypus. Im westlichen Vorort Helsinkis, in Espoo, erweckt dieses Doppelhaus den Eindruck, es habe sich von der sonnigen Riviera hierher verirrt. Dennoch ist es auf eisige finnische Winterverhältnisse vorbereitet: Die filigranen Sprossen der Fenster sitzen in einer Dreifachverglasung. Auf der Südseite sorgt ein System aus vorgelagerten Terrassen, Balkonen und Garagen für zusätzliche Kältepuffer.

Loin de tout cliché de luxe, Erkki Kairamo construit toujours la même sorte de villa, cubique. Dans le faubourg ouest d'Helsinki, à Espoo, cette maison jumelée montre qu'elle serait plus à sa place dans le soleil de la Riviera. Pourtant elle est totalement adaptée aux conditions climatiques finlandaises. Les fins cadres des fenêtres sont pris dans un triple vitrage. Du côté sud, un agencement de terrasses, de balcons et de garages forme un sas contre le froid.

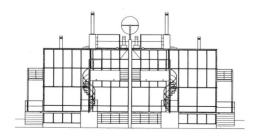

Because sun is a rarity in Finland, a maximum effort is made at obtaining its effects. The house is flooded with light but protected against the cold (triple-glazing). Sketch: Deliberations on the design

Licht und Sonne sind in Finnland Mangelware – deswegen wird alles getan, um sie zur Wirkung kommen zu lassen: Das Haus ist lichtdurchflutet, aber kältegeschützt (Dreifachverglasung). Skizze: Entwurfsüberlegungen des Architekten

On manque toujours de soleil, en Finlande. On fait tout pour le mettre en valeur; la lumière peut circuler dans toute la maison qui est isolée contre le froid (triple vitrage). Esquisse: réflexions d'un architecte

The complex is divided by an urban freeway. The actual shopping centre (above
and drawing) lies to the north of the freeway and the tower is to the south (right
page).

Eine Stadtautobahn zertrennt die Anlage:
Das eigentliche Einkaufszentrum (oben und
Zeichnung) liegt nördlich der Autobahn, der
Turm südlich (rechte Seite).

Une voie urbaine rapide traverse le site: le
centre proprement dit (en haut et dessin)
se trouve au nord, la tour, au sud de la voie
(page de droite).

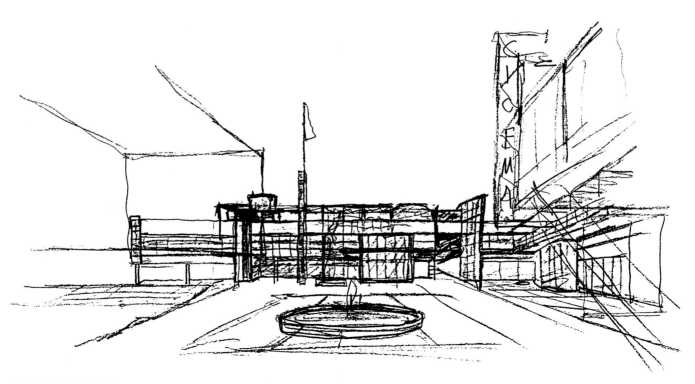

ITÄKESKUS CENTRE 1987
HELSINKI (SF)

The Itäkeskus Centre seeks to make a
mark in Helsinki's uniform suburban
landscape. The conditions were not
very favourable, for the shopping
centre is literally located between a
freeway and subway lines. Nevertheless, the architects succeeded in developing a configuration which, as a
piece of urban design, does justice to
its function as a »centre«. The means
which they used were a tower (with offices), which is particularly effective at
night as an illuminated landmark; as
well as »open« façades of trussed
steel with brick panels.

Das Itäkeskus Centre will in der gleich-
förmigen Vorstadtlandschaft Helsinkis
Zeichen setzen. Die Voraussetzungen
waren nicht günstig, denn das Einkaufszentrum liegt buchstäblich zwischen Autobahnen und Metrolinien.
Dennoch gelingt es den Architekten,
eine städtebauliche Figur zu entwik-
keln, die der Aufgabe »Zentrum« gerecht wird. Die Mittel sind: ein Turm
(mit Büros), der besonders nachts als
illuminierte Landmarke zur Wirkung
kommt, dazu »offene« Fassaden aus
Stahlfachwerk mit Ziegelpaneelen.

Le centre commercial Itäkeskus a l'ambition de marquer le monotone paysage de banlieue, près d'Helsinki, du
sceau de l'originalité. Les conditions
n'étaient guère favorables car ce centre commercial est situé entre autorou-
tes et lignes de métro. Pourtant, les architectes ont réussi une insertion qui
fait que ce «centre» mérite son nom.
Les moyens employés sont: une tour
(de bureaux) qui, la nuit surtout, res-
plendit comme un phare, des façades
«ouvertes» aux structures métalliques
apparentes avec panneaux de brique.

ZAHA **HADID**

Zaha Hadid (*1950 in Baghdad) came onto the scene with a big bang in the early 1980s. She had won the international competition for a clubhouse on the »Peak«, Hong Kong's highest elevation. Her design was not so much reminiscent of a house as of a snapshot of a beast of prey springing from the hillside. The architectural historian, Kenneth Frampton, noted, »the strength of this work rests in the energy-laden flow of space, on the fact that the space which she creates constantly expands, into infinity«. Furthermore, Hadid's work had been shaped by calligraphy. And that was it, for Hadid's success was initially limited to the dissemination of ever new, graphically brilliant drawings. Apart from a small bar in Sapporo, Japan, for a long time none of her designs were actually built. In 1988 she was then part of the small, choice circle of architects celebrated by Philip Johnson in his programmatic »Deconstructivism« exhibition.

Zaha Hadid (*1950 in Bagdad) betrat Anfang der 80er Jahre die Szene mit einem Urknall: Sie hatte den internationalen Wettbewerb für ein Klubhaus am Peak, der höchsten Erhebung in Hongkong, mit einem Gebilde gewonnen, das nicht an ein Haus, sondern an die Momentaufnahme eines aus dem Hang herausspringenden Raubtieres erinnerte. Architekturhistoriker Kenneth Frampton notierte: »Die Stärke dieser Arbeit beruht auf dem energiegeladenen Fließen des Raumes, auf der Tatsache, daß der Raum, den sie schafft, sich immerfort weitet, ins Unendliche hinein«. Ferner: Hadids Arbeit sei kalligraphisch geprägt. Und das war es: Denn Hadids Erfolg beschränkte sich zunächst einmal auf die Verbreitung von immer neuen graphisch brillanten Zeichnungen. Sie baute zunächst nichts, wenn man von einer kleinen Bar in Sapporo, Japan absieht. 1988 gehörte sie dann zu dem kleinen Kreis, den Philip Johnson mit der programmatischen Ausstellung »Dekonstruktivismus« ehrte.

Zaha Hadid (*1950 à Bagdad) a fait une entrée fracassante sur la scène architecturale dans les années 80: elle avait gagné un concours international pour la construction d'un clubhouse sur le Peak, le point le plus haut de Hong-Kong, avec un édifice qui n'avait rien d'une maison mais bien plutôt de l'instantané d'un oiseau de proie décollant du rocher. L'historien Kenneth Frampton, spécialiste d'architecture, écrivit: «La force de ce travail vient du courant d'énergie qui habite l'espace, du fait que l'espace ainsi créé s'étire jusqu'à l'infini.» Il ajoute aussi que le projet de Hadid est marqué par la calligraphie. Et c'était vrai car, dans un premier temps, le succès de Hadid lui vint uniquement de ses dessins, d'un brillant graphisme. A part un petit bar à Sapporo, au Japon, elle ne parvint tout d'abord pas à réaliser de constructions. En 1988, elle fit tout naturellement partie du petit groupe choisi auquel Philip Johnson consacra l'exposition «Déconstructivisme».

Spiral fog or a frozen tornado? Moonsoon
Bar in Sapporo, Japan

Spiralnebel oder eingefrorener Tornado?
Moonsoon-Bar im japanischen Sapporo

Spirale de brume ou tornade figée? Bar
Moonsoon, à Sapporo, au Japon

MOONSOON BAR SAPPORO (J) 1989

Zaha Hadid's work has gone through three phases: the drawing, the rendering in a small form such as furniture or an interior, and finally the building. The Moonsoon Bar can be counted amongst the best examples of the second phase. The furniture and bar are pointed, aggressive, uncomfortable and jut out into a gaudily coloured ambience. It is crowned by a steel structure resembling a tornado frozen in the air.

Zaha Hadids Werk hat drei Phasen durchlaufen: die Zeichnung, die Umsetzung im kleinen überschaubaren Rahmen eines Möbels oder Interieurs und schließlich das Bauwerk. Die Moonsoon-Bar gehört zum besten der Phase zwei. Die Möbel und der Bartresen sind spitz, aggressiv, ungemütlich und ragen in ein grellfarbiges Ambiente: Es wird von einem Stahlenvironment gekrönt, das zu einer Art gefrorenem Tornado im Luftraum wird.

L'œuvre de Zaha Hadid a connu trois phases: le dessin, la traduction à l'échelle réduite d'un meuble ou d'un intérieur et enfin l'œuvre construite. Le Bar Moonsoon se situe au meilleur de la deuxième phase. Les meubles et le comptoir du bar sont pointus, agressifs, inconfortables et l'ambiance est toute de couleurs acides. Pour couronner le tout, un ruban d'acier qui s'élève dans l'espace comme une tornade immobile.

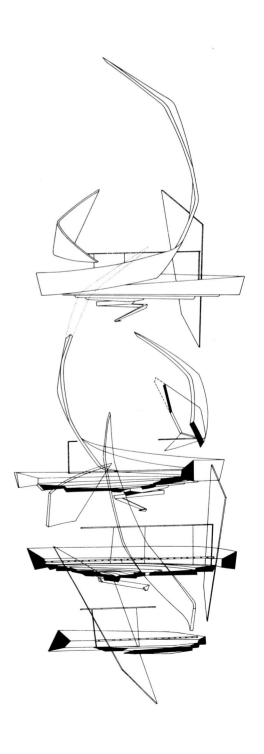

Renunciation of right angles: In the Moonsoon Bar (above: complete view; right page: view onto the actual bar) the barflies are meant to become dizzy. Drawing: (un)systematic depiction of the bar installation

Abstinenz vom rechten Winkel: In der Moonsoon-Bar (oben: Totale; rechte Seite: Blick auf den Tresen) soll es den »Barflies« schwindlig werden. Zeichnung: (un)systematische Darstellung der Barinstallation

Négation de l'angle droit: vue intérieure du Moonsoon Bar (en haut: vue générale; page de droite: vue sur le bar lui-même). Tant pis si les serveuses ont le vertige. Dessin: interprétation de l'agencement du bar

VITRA FIRE-STATION WEIL AM RHEIN (D) 1993

The fire-station, which is also used by the Vitra firm for functions, lies at the end of the main axis running through the firm's site. Here the building takes on »spatial and protective tasks« (Hadid). It greets the visitor with a pointed, arrow-shaped roof. Located underneath the roof is a hall for vehicles, as well as washrooms, changing rooms, a lounge and a fitness room, all of which have been specifically fitted out for the fire brigade. Hadid has arranged them in three so-called »jets«, which shoot dynamically into space. Constructed of reinforced concrete and unframed glass, the house is as minimalist as a building shell. Although this fire-station eschews any semantic statement, because of its implied »speed«, it has an affinity to the theme of »fire brigade«.

Das Feuerwehrhaus, das von der Firma Vitra auch für Veranstaltungen genutzt wird, liegt am Endpunkt der Hauptachse des Firmenareals. Das Haus übernimmt dort »raumbildende und abschirmende Aufgaben« (Hadid). Es empfängt den Besucher mit einem pfeilspitzen Dach, unter dem sich eine Fahrzeughalle und feuerwehrspezifische Einrichtungen wie Naßzellen, Umkleiden, ein Aufenthalts- und ein Fitneßraum befinden. Hadid ordnet sie in sogenannte drei »Strahlen« ein, die dynamisch in den Raum schießen. Das Haus ist minimalistisch wie ein Rohbau – aus Stahlbeton und rahmenlosem Glas. Das Feuerwehrhaus entzieht sich jeder semantischen Aussage und ist trotzdem durch seine angedeutete »Schnelligkeit« sehr nahe am Thema »Feuerwehr«.

Le poste anti-incendie, que l'usine Vitra utilise aussi pour des manifestations exceptionnelles, se trouve à l'extrémité de l'axe principal du site. Il a donc une double fonction «d'obturation et de structuration de l'espace» (Hadid). Le visiteur se trouve devant un toit en forme de flèche qui abrite un hangar pour les véhicules et des installations de prévention de l'incendie ainsi qu'une salle de séjour et une salle de relaxation. Hadid a organisé différentes zones en espaces rayonnants. La construction est minimaliste – béton armé et ouvertures sans cadre. Pas de grandes déclarations sémantiques pour cette création qui pourtant, par son aspect immédiat, évoque la lutte contre le feu.

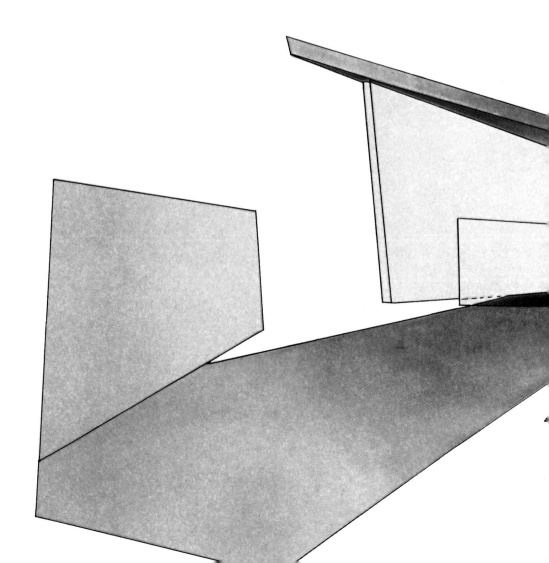

Drawing: exact forecast of an unusual building (see also next page). Above left: lounge in the upper storey. Above right: so-called fitness room on ground floor

Zeichnung: exakte Voraussage eines ungewöhnlichen Bauwerks (vgl. auch nächste Seite). Oben links: Aufenthaltsraum im Obergeschoß. Oben rechts: sogenannter Fitneßraum im Erdgeschoß

Dessin: où une construction peu ordinaire est prévue en détail (voir aussi page suivante). En haut, à gauche: salle de séjour à l'étage. En haut, à droite: salle de relaxation au rez-de chaussée

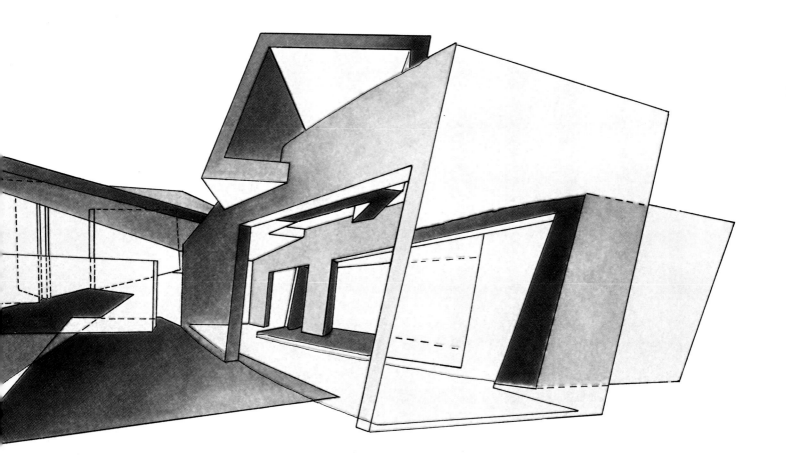

Once more: the forecast and the result, a building between dream and reality

Noch einmal: Voraussage und Ergebnis eines Bauwerks zwischen Traum und Wirklichkeit

Ici encore: prévisions et résultat pour une construction entre rêve et réalité

ADOLF **KRISCHANITZ**

He was born in Pongau (1946) but is a typical Viennese. In his work he has often concerned himself with Vienna's architectural history. He has also derived strength from it, as for example, when he used Loos' Raumplan (plan of volumes) in his housing construction. This meant that even in the publicly subsidized housing in Vienna-Aspern, Krischanitz provided complex, three-dimensional, spatially ingenious floor plans. On the outside these houses are simple. A reason for this might lie in the fact that between 1983 and 1985 he was involved in the painstaking reconstruction of Vienna's Werkbund housing estate. He also does not want to distract with excited citations. »Architecture is not just thinking, not just feeling, not just use; it is far more, the construction of a consciousness through doing. It is a process of continual testing.« Krischanitz belongs to a generation of architects who are no longer only artists and designers but also occupy new positions.

Geboren ist er im Pongau (1946), aber er ist ein typischer Wiener. Er läßt sich immer wieder auf die Wiener Architekturgeschichte ein und zieht aus ihr Kraft, wenn er sich beispielsweise die Raumpläne von Loos für seinen Wohnungsbau zum Vorbild nimmt: Das heißt, selbst im sozialen Wohnungsbau von Wien-Aspern bietet Krischanitz innen komplexe, dreidimensionale, räumlich raffinierte Grundrisse an. Außen sind diese Häuser schlicht. Vielleicht deswegen, weil er sich zwischen 1983 und 1985 mit peniblen Rekonstruktionen der Wiener Werkbundsiedlung beschäftigt hat. Vielleicht auch deswegen, weil er nicht mit aufgeregten Zitaten ablenken möchte.
»Architektur ist nicht nur Denken, nicht nur Fühlen, nicht nur Gebrauch, sie ist vielmehr Aufbau eines Bewußtseins mittels Tun. Sie ist eine fortgesetzte Probe aufs Exempel.« Krischanitz gehört zu einer Generation von Architekten, die nicht mehr nur Künstler und Designer sind, sondern neue Positionen besetzen.

Même s'il est né à Pongau (1946) c'est un vrai Viennois. Il intervient fréquemment sur la scène architecturale de la capitale et c'est d'elle qu'il tire sa force lorsque, par exemple, il s'inspire des plans intérieurs de Loos pour ses appartements. Ce qui signifie que, même dans cette habitation à loyer modéré des faubourgs de Vienne, Krischanitz propose des plans d'appartements complexes, tridimensionnels raffinés. A l'extérieur, ces bâtiments sont simples. Peut-être parce que l'architecte, entre 1983 et 1985, s'est occupé des pénibles travaux de reconstruction de la cité des guildes viennoises. Peut-être aussi parce qu'il ne souhaite pas distraire par des citations architecturales oiseuses. «L'architecture, ce n'est pas seulement une pensée, un sentir, un usage que l'on en fait mais plutôt une conscience obtenue par un acte. C'est une preuve par l'exemple menée à son terme.» Krischanitz fait partie d'une génération d'architectes qui ne sont pas seulement des artistes et des designers.

Insular bridge leading to the temporary exhibition hall on Karlsplatz in Vienna

Rohrbrücke zur temporären Kunst- und Veranstaltungshalle auf dem Wiener Karlsplatz

Passerelle-tunnel menant à l'espace d'expositions et de manifestations artistiques de la Karlsplatz, à Vienne

PILOTENGASSE HOUSING PROJECT VIENNA (A) 1991

The housing project on Pilotengasse in the district of Aspern on Vienna's northern periphery, is a »Central European« undertaking. Together with the Swiss architects, Herzog & de Meuron and the German architect, Otto Steidle, the Austrian Adolf Krischanitz has created housing which »provides maximum comfort with a minimum of expense« (Krischanitz). The housing project's character (the urban design is also by Krischanitz) can be appropriately summed up with the term »plain«. Rendered in plaster, the terraced houses have ingenious lay-outs and are located in narrow alleys and on small squares.

Die Pilotengasse im Stadtteil Aspern an der nördlichen Peripherie Wiens ist ein »mitteleuropäisches« Unternehmen: Zusammen mit den Schweizer Architekten Herzog & de Meuron und dem Deutschen Otto Steidle hat hier der Österreicher Adolf Krischanitz Wohnraum geschaffen, der »bei minimalem Aufwand den maximalen Wohnwert liefert« (Krischanitz).
Der Charakter der Siedlung (städtebaulicher Entwurf ebenfalls Krischanitz) ist mit dem Wort »schlicht« treffend umschrieben: geputzte Reihenhäuser mit formidablen Grundrissen, an schmalen Gassen und kleinen Plätzen.

Le lotissement de la Pilotengasse, à Aspern, dans la banlieue nord de Vienne est une coproduction de trois pays d'Europe centrale. En collaboration avec les architectes suisses Herzog & de Meuron et l'architecte allemand Otto Steidle, l'Autrichien Adolf Krischanitz a créé un habitat qui «avec des moyens minimes offre un confort maximal» (Krischanitz). Le caractère du lotissement (l'étude urbanistique est également de Krischanitz) est, en un mot, «simple». Des maisons mitoyennes crépies, aux plans spacieux, bordent des ruelles étroites et des places exiguës.

200 flats, strung out in long, slightly curved rows (left). Yet the effect is far from boring. Thanks to a clever colour scheme, the roughcast houses have taken on the hues of the rainbow

200 Wohnungen, aufgefädelt an langen, leicht gekrümmten Reihen (links). Trotzdem kommt kaum Langeweile auf: Die Putzbauten sind nach ausgeklügeltem Farbkonzept in Regenbogenfarben gestrichen

200 appartements alignés en longues rangées légèrement courbes (à gauche). Malgré tout, pas de monotonie: les enduits des maisons sont aux couleurs de l'arc-en-ciel, selon un chromatisme recherché

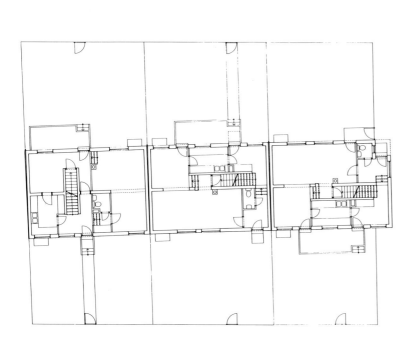

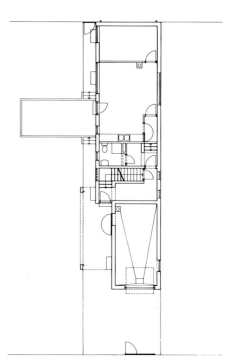

Krischanitz has built single-family homes (above left, and right-hand plan) and terraced houses (right, and left-hand plan). They possess astonishing qualities in terms of space and lay-out, and also boast original surroundings (right)

Krischanitz hat Einzelhäuser (linke Seite und Grundriß rechts) und Reihenhäuser (rechts und Grundriß links) gebaut. Sie verfügen über erstaunliche Raum- und Grundrißqualitäten und ein originelles Umfeld (kleine Bilder ganz rechts)

Krischanitz est l'auteur de maisons individuelles (page de gauche et plan à droite) et de maisons mitoyennes (à droite et plan à gauche). Leur plan et la répartition des espaces sont de grande qualité et leur environnement est original (petites photos à l'extrême droite)

TEMPORARY ART MUSEUM VIENNA (A) 1992

This blue-and-yellow sheet-steel structure on Karlsplatz, a square in the
heart of the Austrian capital, is not a
source of joy to many Viennese. For
them it is simply a foreign body. Krischanitz, on the other hand, had a very
Viennese argument for this harsh
beauty: »There are no disproportion-
ate and senseless parallels drawn with
the powerful walls of this square«. Instead there is an art and exhibition hall
which is as »neutral« as its outer appearance. It is an appropriate, func-
tional structure, fully air-conditioned,
and evenly lit by 39 skilfully distributed
skylights.

Der blaugelbe Stahlblechbau auf dem
Karlsplatz, mitten im Herzen der österreichischen Metropole, bereitet vielen
Wienern wenig Freude – ist er doch
für sie ganz und gar ein Fremdkörper.
Krischanitz argumentiert hingegen für
seine spröde Schönheit ganz wiene-
risch so: »Es gibt keine unverhältnis-
mäßigen und sinnlosen Parallelitäten
mit den mächtigen Platzwänden des
Karlsplatzes.« Dafür existiert eine entsprechend der äußeren Erscheinung
»neutrale« und damit geeignete Nut-
zungsstruktur der voll klimatisierten
und geschickt von 39 Lichtkuppeln
gleichmäßig belichteten Kunst- und
Ausstellungshalle.

La construction métallique bleue et jau-
ne de la Karlsplatz, au cœur de la métropole autrichienne, ne plaît guère
aux Viennois – ils la voient comme un
corps étranger. Krischanitz défend sa
beauté brute avec des arguments typi-
quement viennois: «Elle est sans réfé-
rences et ne crée donc aucune concur-
rence avec les majestueuses façades
de la Karlsplatz.» De plus, elle est une
structure culturelle aussi «neutre» que
son aspect, totalement climatisée et
habilement éclairée par 39 coupoles lu-
mineuses.

The temporary »art container« (left) stands in the shadow of the Karlskirche (right). Drawing: »tubular« bridge, small exhibition hall with coffee-house (below right)

Der »Kunstcontainer« auf Zeit (links) steht im Schatten der Karlskirche (rechts oben); Zeichnung: Rohrbrücke, kleine Ausstellungshalle und Kaffeehaus (rechts unten)

Le «container d'art» temporaire (à gauche) à l'ombre de la Karlskirche (en haut, à droite). Dessin: une passerelle en forme de tunnel, un espace d'exposition et un espace plus réduit avec cafétéria (en bas, à droite)

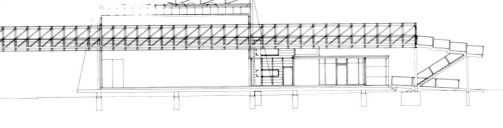

IMRE **MAKOVECZ**

Hungary was the first country in the former Eastern bloc to free itself from old doctrines. An organic architecture was at least a symbolic negation of its unbearable political subordination. Imre Makovecz (* 1935 in Budapest) can be ranked with György Csete as the leading figure in this movement. He has, however, orientated himself more towards Frank Lloyd Wright and Antoni Gaudí than towards strict ideologists such as Hugo Häring and Hermann Finsterlin. Makovecz's approach is anthroposophic. »An organic way of thinking also makes use of the heart; in the conscious sense of the word«, says this architect, whose early houses are all to be understood as components in a revived sense of community. They were communal and cultural buildings or churches. The church in Paks (1987), whose black shingled roof resembles the quivering body of a giant animal, foreshadowed the pavilion in Seville. His architecture is not bound to one style, and is in accordance with nature.

Ungarn war das erste Land des ehemaligen Ostblocks, das sich von alten Doktrinen löste. So wollte es mit einer organischen Architektur die unerträgliche politische Bevormundung zumindest symbolisch aufheben. Imre Makovecz (* 1935 in Budapest) war und ist neben György Csete der Kopf jener Bewegung. Seine Vorbilder sind allerdings eher Frank Lloyd Wright und Antoni Gaudí, weniger die strengen Ideologen wie Hugo Häring oder Hermann Finsterlin. Makovecz' Ansatz ist anthroposophisch: »Die organische Denkweise benutzt auch das Herz im bewußten Sinn des Wortes«, sagt er, dessen frühe Häuser zunächst alle als Glieder wiedererstarkter Dorfgemeinschaften zu verstehen waren: Dorf-, Kultur- oder Gotteshäuser. Die Kirche in Paks (1987), deren Dach aus schwarzen Schindeln wie der bebende Leib eines gigantischen Tieres wirkt, zeigt den Weg zum ungarischen Pavillon in Sevilla (1992). Seine Architektur ist nicht stilgebunden, er baut gemäß der Natur.

La Hongrie fut le premier des pays de l'Est à s'éloigner de toute doctrine. En pratiquant une architecture organique elle souhaitait se libérer, du moins symboliquement, de l'insupportable joug politique. Imre Makovecz (* 1935 à Budapest) fut et reste avec György Csete la figure de proue de ce mouvement. Son inspiration est plus proche de Frank Lloyd Wright et de Antoni Gaudí que de stricts idéologues comme Hugo Häring ou Hermann Finsterlin. Au départ, Makovecz est un anthroposophe: «Le mode de pensée organique fait aussi appel au cœur, au sens conscient du mot», dit-il. Les maisons du début de sa carrière apparurent d'abord comme les éléments de communautés traditionnelles revenues à la vie: maisons villageoises, maisons de la culture ou lieux de culte. L'église de Paks (1987), dont le toit de bardeaux noirs fait penser au corps palpitant de quelque énorme animal, ouvre la voie pour le pavillon hongrois de l'Exposition à Séville. Sa manière n'est pas dépendante d'un style, il procède comme la nature.

»Naturata« (restaurant, store, hotel) in Überlingen. Untreated tree stumps and lami-
nated »branches« are used for the load-
bearing construction

»Naturatá« (Restaurant, Laden, Hotel) in
Überlingen: Unbehandelte Baumstümpfe
und schichtverleimte »Äste« für die Tragkonstruktion

«Naturata» (restaurant, magasin, hôtel) à
Überlingen: troncs d'arbres bruts et «branches» lamellées-collées pour la structure
portante

**NATURATA SHOP RESTAURANT
HOTEL** 1992
ÜBERLINGEN (D)

A health food store, a restaurant and a hotel make up a complex which bears the programmatic name, »Naturata«. Its form is organic, and natural materials have been used. The high peaks on its roof call to mind a child's drawing of a house. The complex frames a small square. »Too many inconsistencies«, wrote a German architectural journal, »will lead a constructively thinking observer to despair.« This complex has to do with other things – namely, »an anthroposophic style of life«.

Naturkostladen, Restaurant und Hotel bilden einen Komplex, der programmatisch »Naturata« heißt – entsprechend organisch die Form und die verwendeten Materialien. Das Haus wirkt mit seinen hohen Dachmützen wie das Abbild einer Urhütte und umrahmt einen kleinen Platz. »Viele Ungereimtheiten«, schrieb eine deutsche Bauzeitung, »bringen den konstruktiv denkenden Betrachter zur Verzweiflung.« Es gehe hier um andere Dinge, nämlich »um eine anthroposophische Lebenshaltung!«

Un magasin de diététique, un restaurant et un hôtel forment le complexe «Naturata», le bien nommé. En conséquence, la forme est organique et le matériau utilisé, naturel. Avec son toit pentu, l'immeuble, construit autour d'une petite place, fait penser à une hutte primitive. «Il y a là suffisamment d'absurdités», écrivit un magazine allemand spécialisé «pour désespérer quelqu'un qui a le sens de la construction.» Mais il s'agit ici d'autre chose, il s'agit «d'une conception anthroposophique de la vie!»

The entrance in the heart of the complex: an almost cultic signal of the Rudolf Steiner movement. The wood in the restaurant and its gallery has been left in its natural state (small pictures)

Das Entree im Herzen der Anlage: ein beinahe kultisches Signal der Rudolf-Steiner-Bewegung. Naturbelassen ist das Holz im Restaurant und dem dazugehörigen Galerieraum (kleine Bilder)

L'entrée, au cœur du complexe, ressemble presque à un lieu de culte, en l'occurrence du mouvement Rudolf Steiner. Dans le restaurant et dans la galerie, le bois a été laissé à l'état naturel (petites photos)

Naturata impressions – as if it were a piece of carefree, natural farmhouse architecture. Below: perspective drawing makes clear the close relationship to archaic farmhouse forms

Naturata-Impressionen – als wär es ein Stück unbekümmerter und urtümlicher Bauernhausarchitektur. Unten: Die Perspektivzeichnung läßt die Nähe zu archaischen Bauernhausformen erkennen

Ambiance naturelle – on se croirait devant un exemple d'architecture paysanne sans prétention. En bas: le dessin permet de voir combien les bâtiments se rapprochent de l'architecture paysanne archaïque

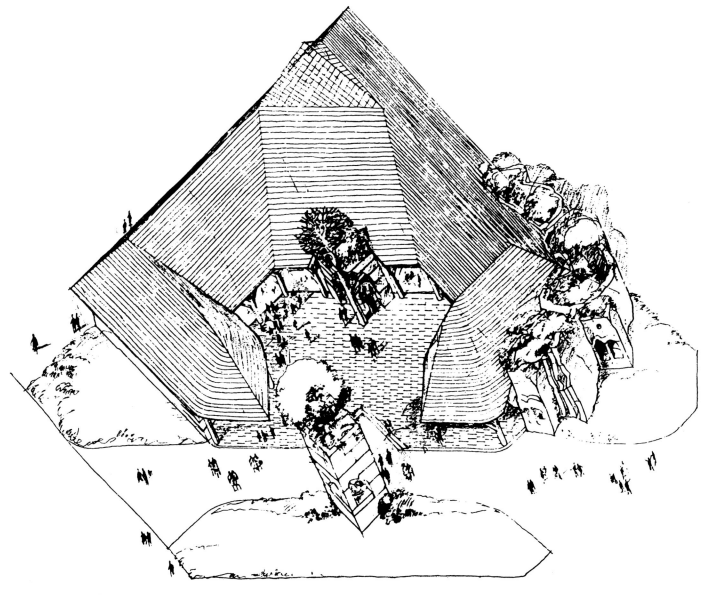

HUNGARIAN PAVILION
SEVILLE (E)

Seven »church towers« push through a slate-clad »hill«. Depending on one's location, the Hungarian pavilion resembles an inhospitable volcanic landscape or an idyllic village setting. This pavilion, with an enormous oak tree at its centre, was the mythic and emotional counterpoint to the generally rationalist presentations of the western industrial nations at Expo 1992. And yet, with his hybrid of church, catacomb and work of art, Makovecz wanted to show above all that Hungary was again participating in Central European culture.

Sieben »Kirchtürme« durchstoßen einen schieferverkleideten »Hügel«. Je nach Standort wirkt der ungarische Pavillon entweder wie eine unwirtliche Vulkanlandschaft oder eine Dorfidylle. Dieser Pavillon mit einem riesigen Lebenseichenbaum in der Mitte war der mythisch-emotionale Kontrapunkt zum meist rationalen Auftritt der westlichen Industrienationen auf der Expo 1992. Und doch wollte Makovecz mit seiner irrationalen Kreuzung aus Kirche, Katakombe und Kunstwerk vor allem gerade eines erreichen: Ungarn wieder als Mitglied einer mitteleuropäischen Kultur zu kennzeichnen.

Sept «clochers» percent une «colline» recouverte d'ardoise. Selon l'angle d'où il est vu, le pavillon apparaît comme un aride paysage volcanique ou un village idyllique. Ce pavillon, avec son énorme arbre de vie en son centre, était le contrepoint mythique et émotionnel d'une performance généralement rationnelle de la part des nations industrialisées, lors de cette Exposition. Pourtant, Makovecz, par cette création tenant à la fois de l'église, de la catacombe et de l'œuvre d'art, voulait justement rattacher la Hongrie à la culture de l'Europe centrale.

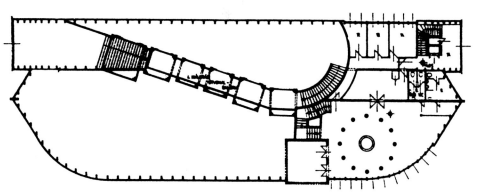

Drawing: a visitor to the pavilion is confronted with the careful staging of a drama. Gorge-like paths lead past the tree of life (above) to the film room (above left) in the »nave«. Right: motifs from Hungarian folk architecture have been intensified to become the architecture of an exhibition pavilion

Zeichnung: Der Besuch des Pavillons ist aufwendig inszeniert wie ein Schauspiel; er führt durch schluchtige Wege, vorbei am Lebensbaum (oben) zum Filmsaal (links oben) im »Kirchenschiff«. Rechts: Motive aus der ungarischen Volksbaukunst, verdichtet zur Architektur eines Ausstellungspavillons

Dessin: la visite du pavillon est aussi précisément mise au point qu'un spectacle. On passe par des galeries profondes auprès d'un arbre de vie (en haut) jusque dans la salle de projection (en haut, à gauche) et dans la «nef». A droite: des thèmes décoratifs du folklore hongrois deviennent architecture pour un pavillon d'exposition internationale

MECANOO

Mecanoo – the name harks back to the metal building kit for children. The nature of Mecanoo's architecture is true to its name. Mecanoo is comprised of four young people: Chris de Weijer (* 1956 in Wageningen), Erick van Egeraat (* 1956 in Amsterdam), Francine Houben (* 1955 in Sittard) and Henk Döll (* 1956 in Haarlem). Mecanoo has continued in the spirit of De Stijl and the International Style which was very influential in Holland (e. g. the van Nelle cocoa factory). Like their predecessors in the Modern Movement, Mecanoo also earned its first plaudits with publicly subsidized housing. In the meantime, however, their architectural language has »recovered from the technical and moral restrictions of the 1920s« (Gerrit Confurius). Their more recent buildings show this development. This also means that their architecture is almost elated, for it combines materials such as wood and glass in a way which would have been a sacrilege fifty years ago.

Mecanoo – der Name erinnert an konstruktives Kinderspielzeug, an einen Metallbaukasten aus vorgegebenen Elementen. Nomen est omen – erklärt er doch das Wesen der Architektur der vier jungen Leute, die hinter Mecanoo stecken: Chris de Weijer (* 1956 in Wageningen), Erick van Egeraat (* 1956 in Amsterdam), Francine Houben (* 1955 in Sittard) und Henk Döll (* 1956 in Haarlem). Mecanoo knüpfen an den Geist von De Stijl und den damals in Holland stark ausgeprägten Internationalen Stil an (z. B. van Nelles Kakao-Fabrik). Ganz wie ihre Altvorderen der Moderne verdienten sich Mecanoo ihre Meriten zunächst im sozialen Wohnungsbau. Die neueren Bauten zeigen: Ihre Architektursprache hat sich inzwischen von »den technischen und moralischen Restriktionen der 20er erholt« (Gerrit Confurius). Das bedeutet auch: Ihre Architektur ist fast beschwingt; sie kombiniert Materialien wie Holz und Glas in einer Weise, die vor fünfzig Jahren als Sakrileg gegolten hätte.

Mecanoo: le nom fait penser à un jeu de construction pour enfants, à des montages d'éléments métalliques préfabriqués. Nomen est omen – celui-ci décrit bien l'architecture des quatre jeunes créateurs qui se cachent derrière Mecanoo: Chris de Weijer (* 1956 à Wageningen), Erick van Egeraat (* 1956 à Amsterdam), Francine Houben (* 1955 à Sittard), Henk Döll (* 1956 à Haarlem). Mecanoo se rattache à l'esprit de De Stijl, l'école internationale qui était jadis particulièrement influente en Hollande (l'usine de cacao van Nelle en est un exemple). Tout à fait comme leurs prédécesseurs modernes, Mecanoo gagna ses premiers galons en réalisant des logements sociaux. Ses constructions récentes démontrent que leur langage architectural s'est libéré, avec le temps, «des astreintes techniques et morales des années 20» (Gerrit Confurius). Cela donne une architecture aérienne, qui mêle des matériaux comme le bois et le verre d'une façon qui, il y a cinquante ans, eût paru sacrilège.

Botanical Institute and library in Wageningen. Stair detail: restrained composition with flair and wit

Botanisches Institut und Bibliothek in Wageningen, Treppendetail: zurückhaltende Komposition mit Spiel und Witz

Institut botanique et bibliothèque à Wageningen, détail de l'escalier: sobre composition d'où l'humour n'est pas absent.

BOOMPJES PAVILION 1990
ROTTERDAM (NL)

In the middle of Rotterdam's rough harbour landscape, where Rem Koolhaas wanted to see the realization of his brave urban utopias, Mecanoo built a restaurant pavilion, as unassuming as it is unconventional. On the harbour side a bold, glass wall slants upwards from gawky concrete legs. On the side facing the city, overlooking a busy street, a wall of natural stone acts as a bulkhead for the building.

Mitten in der rüden Hafenlandschaft Rotterdams, da, wo schon Rem Koolhaas seine mutigen Stadtutopien verwirklichen wollte, baute Mecanoo einen ebenso bescheidenen wie eigenwilligen Restaurantpavillon. Zur Hafenseite steigt schräg eine kühne Glaswand empor, die auf staksigen Betonbeinen steht. Zur Stadtseite, das heißt, zu einer dicht befahrenen Straße hin, schottet sich das Haus mit einer wuchtigen Natursteinwand ab.

Au cœur du rude environnement portuaire de Rotterdam, là où Rem Koolhaas, déjà, avait voulu réaliser ses utopies urbaines, Mecanoo a construit un pavillon-restaurant aussi peu prétentieux qu'original. Du côté port s'élève un mur de verre en plan incliné, porté par de fines jambes de béton. Du côté ville, c'est à dire en bordure d'une rue très fréquentée, le bâtiment se protège d'un massif mur de pierre.

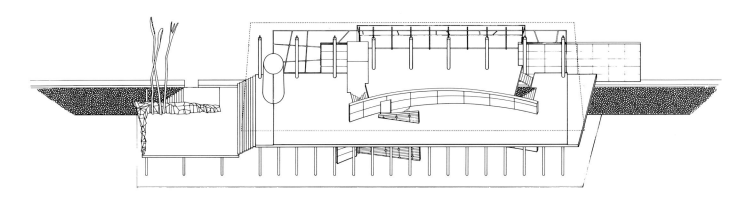

Surprising difference between the exterior (left) and the interior (small pictures); between extremely »cool« and (almost) rustic ambience. »The precise detailing is a reference to the restaurant's good cuisine« (Mecanoo). Below: pavilion with four levels (from bottom to top): WC and entrance, kitchen, café, restaurant

Überraschender Unterschied zwischen außen (links) und innen (kleine Bilder), zwischen ausgesprochen »coolem« und (fast) rustikalem Ambiente: »Die präzise Detaillierung ist eine Referenz an die gute Küche des Restaurants« (Mecanoo). Unten: Pavillon mit vier Ebenen (von unten nach oben): WC und Eingang, Küche, Café, Restaurant

Contraste étonnant entre l'extérieur (à gauche) et l'intérieur (petites photos), entre l'extrêmement sophistiqué et le (presque) rustique: «Le raffinement dans les détails est en correspondance avec la bonne cuisine du restaurant» (Mecanoo). En bas: le pavillon a quatre niveaux (de bas en haut): toilettes et entrée; cuisine; café; restaurant

MECANOO HOUSE 1991
ROTTERDAM (NL)

The house is located between the (artificial) Kralingse Plas lake and a small canal. As far as the structuring of its façade is concerned, the house has been subjected to strict arithmetical rules. Mecanoo has tempered this severity with wood – a congenial building material. On the inside, the skilful way in which three levels have been linked recalls such famous exemplars as those of Adolf Loos or Mies van der Rohe.

Das Wohnhaus steht zwischen dem (künstlichen) See Kralingse Plas und einer kleinen Gracht. Es gehorcht strengen arithmetischen Regeln, soweit es die Gestaltung der Fassade betrifft. Mecanoo mildert die Strenge durch den sympathischen Baustoff Holz ab. Innen verweist die geschickte Verkoppelung der drei Etagen auf bekannte Vorbilder wie von Adolf Loos oder Mies van der Rohe.

Cette maison d'habitation se trouve entre le lac (artificiel) Kralingse Plas et un petit canal. Elle obéit à des règles mathématiques très strictes, du moins en ce qui concerne la façade. Les architectes de Mecanoo ont apporté un adoucissement en utilisant le matériau bois. A l'intérieur, on a fait communiquer les trois étages façon très habile d'Adolf Loos ou de Mies van der Rohe.

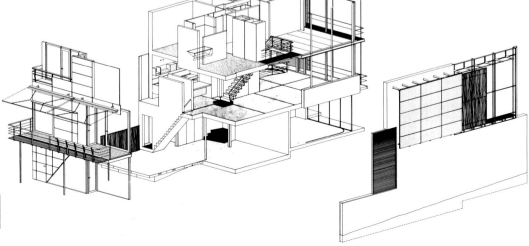

Construction kit logic (above and drawing)
encounters pleasant surroundings and un-
derstated comfort (left page)

Baukastenlogik (oben und Zeichnung) trifft
auf sanfte Gemütlichkeit und angenehmes
Äußeres (linke Seite)

La logique du jeu de construction (en haut
et dessin) rencontre douceur et confort (page de gauche, en bas). Extérieur (page de
gauche, en haut)

MIRALLES Y PINÓS

Despite their youth, their small body of work and a relatively short period of collaboration (1983-92), Carme Pinós (* 1954) and Enric Miralles (* 1955) can be counted amongst the leading figures – perhaps even the cult figures – of the younger generation of European architects. The secret of their success has to do with »being in the right place at the right time«. Miralles y Pinós worked in Barcelona in the galvanizing years after Franco's death. At the time Barcelona had the deserved reputation of being a major centre of design and architecture. In their sensitive treatment of the city's typical architectural requirements – such as the lay-out of the few squares and parks in a sea of houses – they carried on in the tradition and direction of the great Catalan architects, Coderch, Gaudí and Jujol. What is particularly impressive is the way in which they manage to incorporate the site into their architecture. Their buildings are sculptures fashioned out of concrete, stone and soil.

Carme Pinós (* 1954) und Enric Miralles (* 1955) zählen trotz ihres jungen Alters, ihres noch kleinen Werks und einer relativ kurzen Zusammenarbeit (1983-92) bereits zu den Leit-, wenn nicht sogar zu den Kultfiguren der jüngeren europäischen Architektengeneration. Das Geheimnis ihres Erfolgs kann mit »zur rechten Zeit am rechten Ort« umschrieben werden. Miralles y Pinós arbeiteten in der Aufbruchzeit nach Franco in Barcelona, die damals zu Recht als eine der Hauptstädte des Designs und der Architektur galt. Durch ihren sensiblen Umgang mit typischen Bauaufgaben dieser Stadt – wie die Gestaltung der wenigen Plätze und Parks im Häusermeer – haben sie die Tradition und Entwicklungslinie der großen katalanischen Baumeister Coderch, Gaudí und Jujol fortgesetzt. Besonders beeindruckend ist ihre Art, die Topographie des Ortes in ihre Architektur einzubeziehen: Ihre Bauten sind Skulpturen aus Beton, Stein und Erde. Mut und Frische kennzeichnet ihre Arbeit.

Carme Pinós (* 1954) et Enric Miralles (* 1955) comptent malgré leur jeunesse, leur œuvre encore réduite et leur collaboration relativement courte (1983-92) au nombre des plus illustres architectes de la jeune génération européenne. Le secret de leur succès peut être décrit ainsi: «être au bon endroit et au bon moment». Dans l'Espagne de l'après-franquisme, c'est à Barcelone alors considérée à raison comme la capitale du design et de l'architecture, que les deux architectes commencèrent à travailler. La sensibilité qu'ils mirent dans le traitement des problèmes locaux – comme la conception de quelques places et parcs dans une mer d'immeubles – les place dans la lignée des grands maîtres catalans Coderch, Gaudí et Jujol. Ce qui frappe est la façon dont ils font participer la topographie du lieu à leur architecture: leurs constructions sont des sculptures de béton, de pierre et de terre. Ce couple de créateurs a un style plein de courage et de fraîcheur.

Detail of the Igualada cemetery near Barcelona. Rear view of the »shelves« containing the burial chambers

Detail des Friedhofs Igualada bei Barcelona: Rückseite der »Regale«, die die Grabkammern aufnehmen

Détail du cimetière Igualada près de Barcelone: dos des «étagères» dans lesquelles sont placées les caveaux

This cemetery project reveals the affinity of Enric Miralles to Antoni Gaudí, who also blended architectonic and topographic elements in Park Güell into a unique work. It also betrays the influence of Le Corbusier on Carme Pinós. She too makes skilful use of a building's form to achieve special light and shadow effects. The details: the cemetery is a grove, a place for meditation, a peaceful place. Its oval centre is bordered by walls of natural stone. The mausoleums and burial chambers are located behind these walls and below ground. Contrasting elements are the slanted concrete shelves for further burial chambers.

Das Friedhofsprojekt beweist die Geistesverwandschaft von Enric Miralles mit Antoni Gaudí, der im Park Güell gleichermaßen architektonische wie topographische Elemente zu einem einzigartigen Werk zusammenwachsen ließ. Es verrät aber auch den Einfluß von Le Corbusier auf Carme Pinós, die ebenfalls die Form eines Gebäudes für eine spezielle Licht- und Schattenführung geschickt nutzt. Im einzelnen: Der Friedhof ist ein Hain – ein Ort der Meditation, der Ruhe. Im Zentrum liegt ein Oval, begrenzt durch Natursteinmauern: Dahinter und unter der Erde befinden sich Mausoleen und Grabkammern. Kontrastierend dazu nehmen schräggestellte Betonregale weitere Grabstellen auf.

Dans ce projet apparaît la parenté de Enric Miralles avec Antoni Gaudí, qui, au parc Güell, choisit aussi de fondre en une seule œuvre originale les éléments architecturaux et topographiques. Mais il montre également l'influence de Le Corbusier sur Carme Pinós qui, comme lui, détermine la forme du bâtiment en fonction des jeux d'ombre et de lumière. Précisément: le cimetière est un jardin sacré, un lieu de paix. Au centre, un ovale cerné de mur de pierres: derrière ce mur et sous la terre, des mausolées et des caveaux. Des niches de béton dans un plan oblique dans lesquelles sont placés d'autres caveaux contrastent avec l'ensemble.

Above left and right page: as is customary in southern Europe, most of the coffins are placed over and beside each other in a sort of cupboard. Below left: The cemetery's focal point is the oval in its setting of natural stone

Links oben und rechte Seite: Ein Großteil der Särge wird – wie im Süden Europas üblich – in einer Art Schrank über- und nebeneinander verstaut. Unten links: im Mittelpunkt des Friedhofs ein Oval mit einer Einfassung aus Naturstein

En haut, à gauche et page de droite: une grande partie des cercueils sont rangés les uns au-dessus et à côté des autres – comme c'est la coutume en Europe du Sud – dans des sortes d'étagères. En bas, à gauche: au centre du cimetière, un ovale bordé de matériau naturel

Left and right page: great restraint was exercised in fashioning the chapel and its adjoining rooms. Its round walls correspond to the topography of the cemetery as a whole – and to the central oval (see drawing)

Links und rechte Seite: Die Kapelle und ihre Nebenräume wurden äußerst zurückhaltend gestaltet. Ihre runden Wände korrespondieren mit der Topographie der gesamten Friedhofsanlage – wie dem zentralen Oval (vgl. Zeichnung)

A gauche et page de droite: la chapelle et ses espaces annexes sont d'une conception très sobre. Ses murs arrondis correspondent avec la topographie générale du lieu, tout comme l'ovale qui se trouve au centre (voir dessin)

ARCHERY RANGE BARCELONA (E) 1992

As with the Igualada cemetery, the archery range for the Olympic Games in Hebron Valley (Barcelona) is remarkable for the way in which the existing terrain has been incorporated into the concept as a whole. The facilities containing changing rooms and supplies for the athletes are located under vaulted prefabricated concrete elements which lie crosswise to each other. Like the neighbouring housing, they seem to have been arranged according to pure chance and therefore they too make a lively impression.

Wie der Friedhof Igualada zeichnet sich die olympische Wettkampfanlage für die Bogenschützen im Vall de Hebron (Barcelona) vor allem dadurch aus, daß das vorhandene Terrain in die Gesamtkonzeption einbezogen wird. Die Umkleideanlagen und Versorgungseinrichtungen für Sportler liegen unter gegeneinander verschränkten und gewölbten Betonfertigteilen. Sie wirken ähnlich zufällig zusammengestellt und dadurch lebendig wie die benachbarte Wohnbebauung.

Comme le cimetière Igualada, le terrain olympique de tir à l'arc de Vallée de Hebron (Barcelone) se caractérise par une insertion réussie dans l'environnement. Les cabines et les diverses installations sportives se trouvent placées sous des éléments préfabriqués de béton reliés les uns aux autres. On a l'impression qu'ils ont été posés là au hasard. Le résultat en est très vivant, aussi vivant que les lotissements voisins.

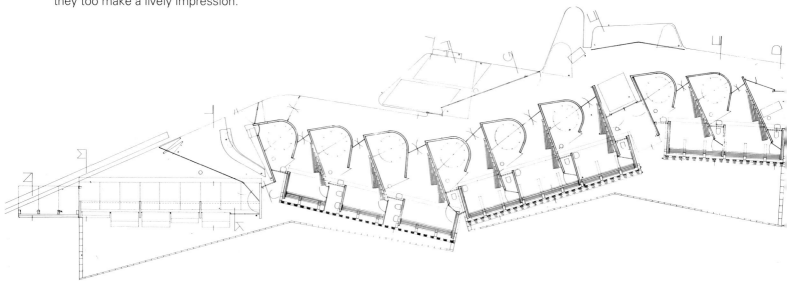

The necessary facilities for the athletes on the Olympic archery range disappeared behind large concrete walls (below). The red concrete is also visible on the inside (right). Drawing: the changing room facilities and adjoining rooms are partly underground

Die notwendigen Einrichtungen für die Sportler auf den olympischen Bogenschützenanlagen verschwinden hinter großen Betonwänden (unten). Auch innen bleibt der rohe Beton sichtbar (rechts). Zeichnung: Die Umkleideanlagen und Nebenräume graben sich zum Teil in den Erdboden ein

Les installations indispensables aux tireurs à l'arc olympiques disparaissent derrière de grands murs de béton (en dessous). A l'intérieur aussi, le béton est à nu (à droite). Dessin: les cabines de déshabillage et les annexes se trouvent en partie au sous-sol

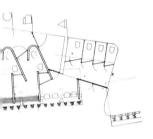

JEAN **NOUVEL**

»A building should impart a sense of what moved an epoch!« Jean Nouvel (* 1945 in Fumel) has remained true to his basic principle. No other architect has been as consistent and as accurate in building the Zeitgeist. It is with good reason that he is considered to be a High Tech architect, but his rendering of this style is more restrained and poetic than that of his British counterparts. A socialist and early starter (at the age of 23 he was already responsible for the construction of 80 apartments in Neuilly), Nouvel's entrance ticket to the world of mega-architects was his Institut du Monde arabe in Paris (1987). In the following years Nouvel increasingly developed his own style. It is particularly in German cities like Cologne, Berlin or Frankfurt that he has transformed buildings into canvases. Nouvel is already working on his own monument: the Tour Sans Fins. At 420 meters, it will storm the heavens at La Défense in Paris.

Seinen Leitsatz: »Ein Gebäude soll spüren lassen, was eine Epoche bewegt!« ist Jean Nouvel (* 1945 in Fumel) treu geblieben. Kein anderer Architekt baut so konsequent und korrekt den Zeitgeist wie Nouvel. Nicht zu Unrecht wird er dem High-Tech zugeordnet, setzt es aber sanfter und poetischer als seine britischen Kollegen um. Der Sozialist und Frühstarter Nouvel (er verantwortete schon mit 23 Jahren in Neuilly den Bau von 80 Wohnungen) löste seine Eintrittskarte in die Welt der Megaarchitekten 1987 mit der Vollendung des Institut du Monde arabe in Paris. In der Folge findet Nouvel immer mehr seinen persönlichen Stil. Besonders in deutschen Städten wie Frankfurt, Köln oder Berlin. Dort werden Häuser zu »Leinwänden«, deren Glasfassaden mit neuester Siebdrucktechnik Botschaften aussenden. Und sein eigenes Denkmal hat er auch schon in Arbeit: der Tour Sans Fins, ein Himmelstürmer von 420 Metern Höhe in Paris – La Défense.

Sa devise est: «Un bâtiment doit donner à sentir les soubresauts d'une époque» et Jean Nouvel (* 1945 à Fumel) y est resté fidèle. Aucun autre architecte ne recrée de façon aussi juste et aussi cohérente l'esprit de son temps. On le compte, et pas à tort, au nombre des créateurs High Tech, mais sa manière est plus douce et plus poétique que celle de ses confrères anglais. Socialiste, débutant précoce (à 23 ans il fut responsable de la construction de 80 appartements à Neuilly), il fit son entrée dans le monde des Tout Grands en 1987 avec son Institut du Monde arabe, à Paris. Par la suite, il réalise davantage l'adéquation entre son style et son époque, surtout à Francfort, Cologne ou Berlin. Il y construit des maisons-écrans dont les façades diffusent l'information grâce à la technique la plus moderne. Il travaille déjà à son propre monument: la Tour Sans Fins, un gratteciel de 420 m dans le quartier de la Défense, à Paris.

Wall detail on the residential building in Nîmes. Jean Nouvel prefers High Tech materials

Wanddetail am Wohnhaus in Nîmes: Jean Nouvel bevorzugt High-Tech-Materialien

Détail d'un mur d'une maison à Nîmes: Jean Nouvel privilégie les matériaux High Tech

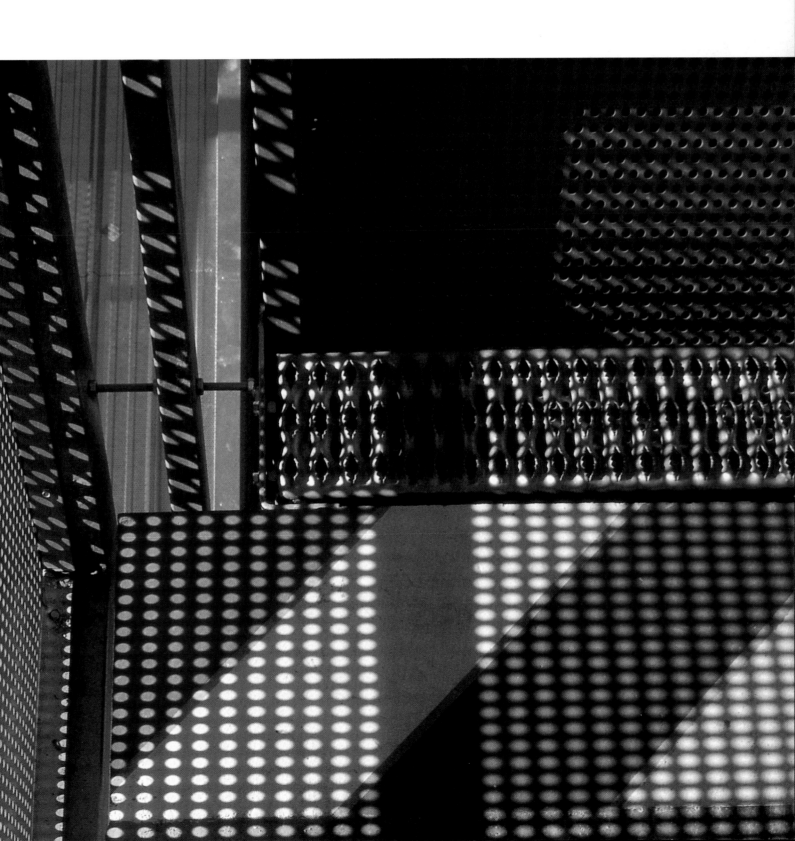

NEMAUSUS NÎMES (F) 1987

Concealed behind this unusual name and the equally distinctive »metal dress« is Nouvel's successful attempt to show that he belongs to social housing's most experimental architects. This new type of »machine for living« has plans which are surprisingly neutral in their assigned use. Spread up to three storeys, they allow families to determine the specific lay-out of their flats. »Abundance of space« is how Nouvel describes what he has provided here in 17 variations for 114 flats. And when one looks more closely at the »inhospitable machine aesthetic« one sees that it makes ecological sense. In the generally sunny climate of Nîmes protective devices against the sun are an absolute necessity.

Hinter dem ungewöhnlichen Namen und dem ebenso unverwechselbaren »Blechkleid« verbirgt sich der gelungene Nachweis Nouvels, zu den experimentierfreudigsten Architekten des sozialen Wohnungsbaus zu gehören. Dieser neue Typus einer »Wohnmaschine« verfügt über überraschend nutzungsneutrale Grundrisse, die auf bis zu drei Ebenen den Familien individuelle Wohngestaltung ermöglichen: »Überfluß an Raum« nennt Nouvel, was er dort in 17 Variationen für 114 Wohnungen vorsieht. Und die »menschenfeindliche Maschinenästhetik« löst sich beim näheren Hinsehen als ökologisch sinnvoll auf: Im meist sonnigwarmen Klima von Nîmes sind Sonnenschutzeinrichtungen notwendig.

Sous ce nom étrange et sous le caractéristique revêtement de métal se cache une réalisation qui met Nouvel au rang des architectes de logements sociaux les plus originaux. A ce nouveau type de «machine à habiter» correspondent des plans où la répartition de l'espace est étonnamment neutre et qui permettent aux familles, parfois sur trois niveaux, de structurer elles-mêmes leur cadre de vie. «Surabondance d'espace», dit Nouvel pour décrire les 17 variations qu'il a créées pour les 114 appartements. L'«inhumaine esthétique de la machine» laisse place, à y regarder de plus près, à un bon sens écologique: dans le climat le plus souvent chaud de Nîmes les protections contre le soleil sont indispensables.

Dwellings in the setting of an express train (above: front of train, right: back of train)

Wohnen in den Kulissen eines Expreßzuges (oben: Zugnase, rechts: Zugende)

Vivre dans les coulisses d'un train rapide (en haut: tête du train, à droite, queue du train)

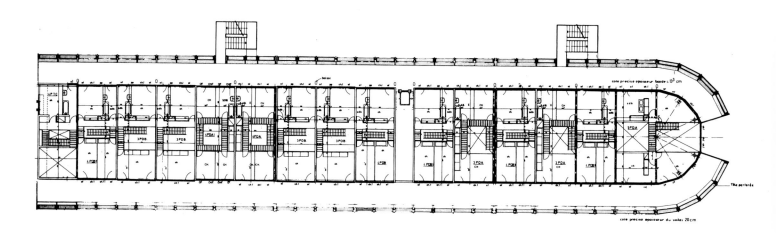

Although the plan also recalls the way that railway compartments are strung together, the flats are very luxurious and are lit on several levels (see right) from two sides. Right page: the hallways have been fitted out to a minimalist standard, but this does not detract from the overall quality

Der Grundriß erinnert ebenfalls an die Aneinanderreihung von Zugabteilen; die Wohnungen sind aber sehr luxuriös: auf mehreren Ebenen (vgl. rechts) von zwei Seiten belichtet. Rechte Seite: Minimalistischer Ausbaustandard in den Fluren mindert die Wohnqualität nicht

Le plan rappelle une succession de compartiments mais les appartements sont luxueux: sur plusieurs niveaux (voir à droite) ils sont éclairés par deux côtés. Page de droite: l'équipement minimaliste des couloirs ne diminue en rien la qualité de l'habitat

The IMA is one of France's »Grands Projets de l'Etat«. To this point it is also Nouvel's most important building. It contains a museum, a library and documentation centre, an auditorium and a restaurant looking out over the roofs of Paris. The IMA is the »showroom« of Arab culture in the West and was designed accordingly by Nouvel. Rich treasures from the Arab world lie in technoid display cases. On the outside of the building, aluminium, glass and concrete have been welded together to create a building which bears witness to a fantastic level of technological expertise.

Das IMA zählt zu den »Grands Projets de l'Etat« Frankreichs. Es ist auch Nouvels bisher wichtigstes Bauwerk und enthält ein Museum, eine Bibliothek und ein Dokumentationszentrum, ein Auditorium und ein Restaurant über den Dächern von Paris. Das IMA ist der »showroom« der arabischen Kultur im Westen, und entsprechend wurde es von Nouvel gestaltet: Güldene arabische Pretiosen liegen in technoiden Vitrinen; Aluminium, Glas und Beton werden außen zu einem Baukörper zusammengeschweißt, der von einem phantastischen technischen Leistungsstand kündet.

L'IMA compte au nombre des «Grands Projets» de l'Etat français. C'est aussi, à ce jour, la création la plus importante de Nouvel. L'édifice contient un musée, une bibliothèque et un centre de documentation, un auditorium et un restaurant avec vue sur les toits de Paris. L'IMA est la «vitrine» de la culture arabe en Occident et c'est ainsi qu'il a été conçu par l'architecte: de riches trésors arabes sont présentés dans des transparences très étudiées. À l'extérieur l'aluminium, le verre et le béton ont été assemblés en un édifice qui est une véritable prouesse technique.

A »canyon« separates the glass projection for the museum and exhibition area from the other rooms (right and drawing). Right page: a High Tech control system alters the size and shape of the diaphragms, creates different lighting conditions and offers protection from the sun

Eine »Schlucht« trennt die gläserne Nase für Museum und Ausstellungsbereich von den übrigen Räumen (rechts und Zeichnung). Rechte Seite: Eine High-Tech-Steuerung verändert Größe und Form der Diaphragmen und sorgt für wechselnde Lichtstimmung und Sonnenschutz

Une «faille» sépare l'avancée de verre du musée des autres salles (à droite et dessin). Page de droite: une centrale électronique modifie taille et forme des diaphragmes, permettant des variations d'éclairage et une protection du soleil

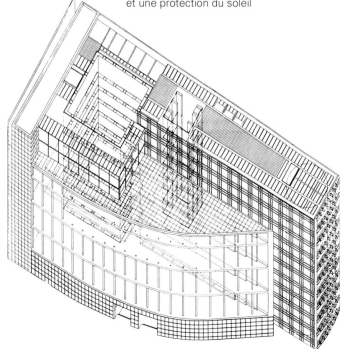

HOTEL DES THERMES DAX (F) 1992

The new hotel in Dax also forges links between yesterday and today. It is a square block under a vaguely wing-like roof. The inside and outside have a rhythmically articulated metal façade into which the wooden shutters typical of the area have been inserted. Pergolas lead to the hotel rooms which are grouped around an air well. The latter extends for the height of the building and contains the thermal pool. All in all, a building was created which could always have been standing here. This impression can only be sustained, however, if one does not look too carefully at its clever technical details.

Auch das neue Hotel in Dax versucht, Brücken zwischen gestern und heute zu schlagen. Das Haus in Form eines Quaders unter der Andeutung eines Flugdaches besteht innen und außen aus einer rhythmisch gegliederten Metallfassade, in die die ortstypischen Holzschlagläden eingefügt sind. Die Hotelzimmer werden durch Laubengänge erschlossen und gruppieren sich um einen haushohen Lichthof, in den das Thermalschwimmbecken eingefügt worden ist. Alles zusammengenommen, ist ein Gebäude entstanden, das hier schon immer hätte stehen können – allerdings nur, wenn man die ausgefuchsten technischen Details außer acht läßt.

Le nouvel hôtel de Dax se veut, lui aussi, un pont entre hier et aujourd'hui. La maison, rectangulaire et coiffée d'un toit légèrement ondulé présente à l'intérieur et à l'extérieur une façade de métal au motif répétitif dans laquelle sont inclus les volets de bois traditionnels. Les chambres de l'hôtel s'ouvrent sur des tonnelles autour d'une cour intérieure incluant le bassin thermal. En conclusion, ce qui a été réalisé ici est une construction qui aurait toujours pu s'y trouver – détails techniques mis à part.

Exhilarating, transparent, light – the overall impression made by the hotel (right page above). The interior offers the comfort of a grand hotel (right) with a thermal pool (right page below)

Beschwingt, transparent, leicht – der Gesamteindruck des Hotels (rechte Seite oben). Innen der Komfort eines Grandhotels (rechts) mit ovalem Thermalbecken (rechte Seite unten)

Dynamique, transparente, légère, telle est l'impression que donne l'hôtel (page de droite, en haut). A l'intérieur, le confort d'un grand hôtel (à droite) et un bassin thermal ovale (page de droite, en bas)

PAOLO **PORTOGHESI**

The role which Robert Venturi played in American Post-Modernism was played in Italy, or even in Europe, by Paolo Portoghesi (* 1931 in Rome). He is a seminal thinker and pioneer. His manifesto stands in Rome. The Casa Baldi (1959), a villa with the vigour of the Italian Baroque, »places the mere game of modernistic sweeping lines and curves into a cultural context« (Heinrich Klotz). Years later Portoghesi became the director of the Biennale of architecture, whose 1980 exhibition »The Presence of the Past« sanctioned the Post-Modern movement in Europe. He subsequently made a name for himself as a historian and critic. With a mosque that he built in Rome in 1976 he placed his theme of »architectural renewal in the lap of history« in the overlapping context of two religions. Elements of baroque Rome are combined with those from the Eastern world of Mecca and Medina. It is a spectacle of quite a different nature than Nouvel's Institut du Monde arabe in Paris.

Was Robert Venturi für die amerikanische Postmoderne ist, das ist Paolo Portoghesi (* 1931 in Rom) für Italien, ja für Europa: Vordenker und Wegbereiter. Sein gebautes Manifest steht in Rom: die Casa Baldi (1959), eine Villa mit der vitalen Kraft des italienischen Barock, die »das bloße Spiel modernistischer Linienschwünge und Kurven in einen kulturellen Kontext setzt« (Heinrich Klotz). Jahre später wurde Portoghesi Direktor der Architekturbiennale in Venedig, die 1980 mit der Ausstellung »The Presence of the Past« die Postmoderne in Europa sanktionierte. Danach machte er sich als Historiker und Kritiker einen Namen. Mit einer Moschee in Rom hat er 1976 sein eigenes Thema »Erneuerung der Architektur im Schoße der Geschichte« in einen übergreifenden Kontext zwischen zwei Religionen gestellt: Kombinationen aus dem barocken Rom mit der orientalischen Welt von Mekka und Medina – ein Spektakel ganz anderer Art als Nouvels Institut du Monde arabe in Paris.

Ce qu'est Robert Venturi aux postmodernes américains, Paolo Portoghesi (* 1931 à Rome) l'est pour l'Italie, et même l'Europe: un théoricien avancé et un pionnier de ce mouvement. Son édifice-manifeste se trouve à Rome: c'est la Casa Baldi (1959), une villa qui possède la force vitale du baroque italien et qui «situe dans un contexte culturel le simple jeu du mouvement des lignes et des courbes propre à l'architecture moderne» (Heinrich Klotz). Des années plus tard, Portoghesi devint directeur de la Biennale qui, en 1980, officialisa le mouvement postmoderne européen avec l'exposition «The Presence of the Past». Ensuite il se fit un nom comme historien et critique. En 1976, avec la construction d'une mosquée à Rome il plaça le thème, «renouvellement de l'architecture dans le sein de l'histoire», dans un contexte commun. Cette combinaison de la Rome baroque et du monde oriental de la Mecque et de Médine donne un tout autre résultat que l'Institut du Monde arabe de Nouvel.

Paolo Portoghesi as a master of ornamentation – staircase seen from below in the Palazzo Corrodi in Rome

Paolo Portoghesi als Meister des Ornaments – Treppenuntersicht im Palazzo Corrodi in Rom

Paolo Portoghesi, maître de l'ornement – vue de dessous de l'escalier dans le Palazzo Corrodi à Rome

MOSQUE AND ISLAMIC CENTRE

ROME (I) 1976

It is indubitably one of the more difficult architectural tasks to build an Islamic centre in the middle of Rome. The architects (Paolo Portoghesi with Vittorio Gigliotti and Sami Mousawi) solved this problem with bravura by adroitly bringing together two cultures in one building. They used variations of Islamic motifs, innovative and more than mere copies. At the same time the building's centre recalls the European Baroque and Rome's architectural history.

Es gehört sicher zu den schwierigeren Bauaufgaben, mitten in Rom ein islamisches Zentrum zu bauen. Die Architekten (Paolo Portoghesi mit Vittorio Gigliotti und Sami Mousawi) haben sie mit Bravour gelöst, weil sie beide Kulturen in einem Bauwerk gekonnt zusammenführen. Dabei wenden sie Variationen islamischer Motive an, die innovativ und mehr als bloße Kopien sind. Gleichzeitig wird durch die bauliche Figur des Zentrums an die Zeit des europäischen Barock und die Baugeschichte der Stadt Rom erinnert.

Il n'est guère facile de constuire un centre islamique en plein Rome. Les architectes (Paolo Portoghesi en collaboration avec Vittorio Gigliotti et Sami Mousawi) s'en tirent avec les honneurs en traitant les deux cultures en un seul bâtiment. Ils utilisent pour cela des variations de thèmes islamiques de façon innovante. En même temps, la silhouette de l'édifice agit comme un rappel du baroque européen et de l'histoire architecturale de la ville.

Left: Minaret and mosque stand out above. A congress centre with adjoining rooms is located under the colonnade (see also plan). Above: light and shadow as structual elements – as in the Orient

Links: Minarett und Moschee überragen das islamische Zentrum. Unter dem Säulengang liegen ein Kongreßzentrum mit Nebenräumen (vgl. auch Grundriß). Oben: Licht und Schatten gestalten mit – wie im Orient

A gauche: minaret et mosquée dominent le centre islamique. Sous la colonnade se trouve un centre des congrès avec ses salles adjacentes (voir aussi plan). En haut: lumière et ombre comme éléments structurants – comme en Orient

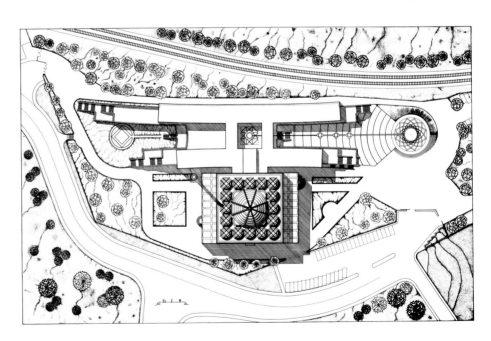

In the mosque a forest of columns supports the dome -»the circle is the symbol of the heavens and of order«

In der Moschee trägt ein Wald aus Säulen die Kuppel – der »Kreis ist Symbol des Himmels und der Ordnung«

Dans la mosquée, une forêt de colonnes portent la coupole – le «cercle est le symbole du céleste et de l'ordre»

Sensitive urban renewal: the architecture is new but it seems as if it has always been there. Right page: the tower is the symbol of the Italian city

Sensible Stadterneuerung – die Architektur ist neu und wirkt so, als sei sie immer dort gewesen. Rechte Seite: Wahrzeichen der italienischen Stadt ist der Turm

Rénovation urbaine pleine de subtilité. Les bâtiments sont nouveaux et semblent avoir toujours été là. Page de droite: signal d'une ville italienne, la tour

CIVIC SQUARE 1986
POGGIOREALE (I)

The »piazza« is an Italian export to cities all over the world. It has already found a place in New Orleans and will soon be found on Potsdamer Platz in Berlin. In the Sicilian city of Poggioreale, Portoghesi used the piazza as an »ordering factor and figure« in the construction of a new urban centre. It is framed by a sweeping two-storeyed colonnade and by the social, cultural and commercial facilities typical of a small town.

Die »Piazza« hat sich als italienischer Architekturexport in Städten der ganzen Welt etabliert: In New Orleans genauso wie demnächst am Potsdamer Platz in Berlin. In der sizilianischen Stadt Poggioreale benutzt Portoghesi die Piazza als »Ordnungsfaktor und -figur« für den Bau eines neuen Stadtzentrums. Sie wird eingefaßt durch einen schwungvollen doppelstöckigen Säulengang und soziale, kulturelle und kommerzielle Einrichtungen einer Kleinstadt.

L'Italie a exporté sa «piazza» dans le monde entier: à New Orleans comme, bientôt, à Berlin, Potsdamer Platz. A Poggioreale, en Sicile, Portoghesi en fait un «facteur d'ordre, une forme signifiante» dans la conception d'un nouveau centre-ville. Elle y est entourée d'une colonnade à étage très dynamique et des éléments socio-culturels et commerciaux propres à une petite ville.

SJOERD **SOETERS**

»Amongst Holland's architects, Sjoerd Soeters (* 1947 on Ameland) is the cheekiest boy in the class« (Ruud Brouwers). One can best understand how this smug accusation is meant when one looks at the technically perfect houses of other Dutch architects (e. g. Mecanoo). When Soeters is taken seriously, however, and placed in a historical context, it becomes clear that he is representative of a pluralist tendency in 20th century Dutch architecture. It manifested itself in the Expressionist Amsterdam School, which has always been antipodal to the purism of De Stijl. It would be tragic and superficial to use the term »Post-Modern« architecture once again. His cinema and games arcade in Zandvoort is of course a variation on the »decorated shed« (Robert Venturi). His designs for his own office and the building for the Ministry of Transport and Communications reveal his careful hand and his competence in working with space and material.

»Unter den holländischen Architekten ist Sjoerd Soeters (* 1947 auf Ameland) der frechste Bursche in der Klasse« (Ruud Brouwers). Man versteht diese süffisante Anklage insbesondere dann, wenn man sich die sachlich perfekten Häuser anderer holländischer Architekten (z. B. Mecanoo) anschaut. Historisch und seriös betrachtet, verkörpert Soeters jedoch nur das »Sowohl-als-auch« in der niederländischen Architektur des 20. Jahrhunderts, in der es mit der expressiven Amsterdamer Schule immer schon ein Gegenstück zum Purismus des De Stijl gab. Es wäre tragisch und oberflächlich, wieder einmal nur von postmoderner Architektur zu sprechen. Natürlich sind sein Kino und die Spielhalle in Zandvoort eine Variante des »dekorierten Schuppens« (Robert Venturi). Seine Entwürfe für das eigene Büro und das Ministerium für Transport und Kommunikation beweisen, daß er ein sorgfältiger Gestalter ist, kompetent für Raum und Material.

«Parmi les architectes hollandais, Sjoerd Soeters (* 1947 à Ameland) est l'élève le plus dissipé de la classe» (Ruud Brouwers). On comprend surtout cette accusation un peu facile lorsqu'on fait la comparaison avec les constructions des autres architectes hollandais (celles de Mecanoo, par exemple). Plus sérieusement, et d'un point de vue historique, si Soeters représente le «n'importe quoi» de l'architecture des Pays-Bas c'est surtout parce que la très expressive école d'Amsterdam a toujours été le pendant des purs et durs du mouvement De Stijl. Ce serait en effet tragique et superficiel, que de parler une fois encore à son égard d'architecture postmoderne. Bien sûr, son cinéma et la salle de jeux de Zandvoort son une variation sur le thème du «hangar décoré» (Robert Venturi). Ses projets pour sa propre agence, pour plusieurs maisons d'habitation et le Ministère des transports prouvent qu'il est un concepteur solide, avec des compétences particulières dans la gestion de l'espace et des matériaux.

The colourful world of Sjoerd Soeters: load-bearing construction for the »Zandvoort Circus«

Die bunte Welt des Sjoerd Soeters: Tragkonstruktion des Zandvoort Circus

Le monde fantaisiste de Sjoerd Soeters: structure portante du Zandvoort Circus

CIRCUS ZANDVOORT (NL) 1986

Were the façade not decorated to look like the tricolour of the Netherlands, this passing recollection of the architecture of seafarers and circus performers could be understood as a part of an American »main street«. And indeed, it is a »home« to video games, slot-machines and a cinema with so-called »love seats«. The building is correspondingly frivolous, ephemeral and imaginative. Some might call this Post-Modern. A better appraisal is »appropriate to its purpose«.

Würde nicht die niederländische Tricolore als Fassadenschmuck grüßen, könnte man diese flüchtige Erinnerung an die Architektur der Fahrens- und Zirkusleute auch als Stück einer amerikanischen »Mainstreet« begreifen: Es handelt sich um ein »Home« für Videospiele, Slot machines und ein Kino mit sogenannten »love seats«, und entsprechend frivol, vorläufig und phantasievoll ist das Bauwerk. Manche mögen das postmodern nennen. Besser lautete das Urteil »dem Zweck angemessen«.

Si le drapeau tricolore néerlandais n'en décorait pas la façade, cette construction, qui fait allusion à l'architecture des gens du voyage, évoquerait plutôt la rue principale d'une petite ville provinciale américaine: elle abrite des jeux vidéo, des machines à sous et un cinéma pourvu de «love seats». Le style en est donc frivole, éphémère et plein de poésie. Certains diront qu'il est postmoderne. Il faudrait plutôt dire: adapté à sa fonction.

From the left: portal to the two-storeyed hall; cinema (behind an outsize flag of the Netherlands). On the inside, the video games for »family entertainment« are below, the »slots« above

Von links: Portal zur zweistöckigen Halle; Kino (hinter einer überdimensionalen niederländischen Flagge). Innen stehen die »familiengerechten« Spielautomaten unten, die »slots« oben

De gauche à droite: accès aux deux niveaux; cinéma (derrière le gigantesque drapeau néerlandais). A l'intérieur, les jeux «pour tous publics» sont en bas, les machines à sous, en haut

MINISTRY OF TRANSPORT AND COMMUNICATIONS THE HAGUE (NL) 1990

A former KLM office of the 1940s was turned into a ministerial building in 1971. Within the scope of an extensive renovation process, Soeters was commissioned with two projects: a new access road with entrance and the actual ministerial wing. With the latter Soeters showed his strengths: the differentiated lay-out of distinct areas. He dissolved the existing hallway structure, put in slanted and curved walls and dug into the depths of the old ceiling construction: the new alternative office scheme.

Ein früheres KLM-Büro aus den 40er Jahren, wurde 1971 zum Ministeriumsgebäude. Soeters bekam im Rahmen einer umfangreichen Renovierung zwei Teilaufträge: eine neue Zufahrt mit Eingang und den eigentlichen Ministertrakt. Dort zeigt Soeters seine Stärken: die differenzierte Gestaltung von übersichtlichen Bereichen. Er löst die alte Flurstruktur auf, zieht schräge und gekurvte Wände ein und gräbt sich in die Tiefen der alten Deckenkonstruktion ein. Die Neugeburt eines alternativen Büroschemas.

Un ancien immeuble de la KLM des années 40 devint ministère en 1971. Dans le cadre d'une rénovation générale, Soeters fut chargé d'intervenir sur deux points: d'abord, construction d'un nouvel accès pour voitures avec une entrée, création d'espaces pour le ministère proprement dit. C'est là, dans le domaine de la structuration de l'espace que Soeters s'illustre. Il efface les anciennes divisions, élève de nouveaux murs, en biais, en courbes et surélève les plafonds: c'est une renaissance pour des bureaux originaux.

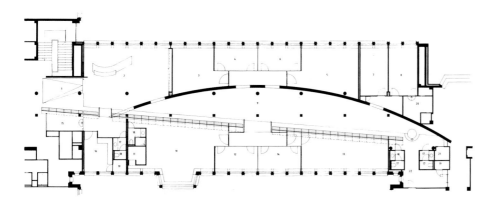

Left, left page: the access road. A slanted point of view in the ministerial tract (centre). The same wall also shields the large conference room (above). Drawing: plan of the ministerial wing

Linke Seite links: Schwung in der Zufahrt. Schräge Regie im Ministertrakt (Mitte). Dieselbe Wand gibt Deckung für den großen Besprechungsraum (oben). Zeichnung: Grundriß des Ministertrakts

Page de gauche, à gauche: rampe d'accès dynamique. Choix de l'oblique pour les quartiers ministériels (milieu). Le même mur abrite une salle de réunion (en haut). Dessin: plan des quartiers ministériels

Ministerial area. The old grid for the girders no longer seems to play a load-bearing role. They give the impression of prancing pillars. The visual effects are produced on the one side by the curved wall and on the other side by a slanting, semi-transparent wall which has carved itself into a tiled hollow opening in the floor. Despite the apparently infinite variety of materials, Soeters has retained control and the ambience still remains exciting

Ministerbereich. Das alte Raster der Stützen scheint keine tragende Rolle mehr zu spielen; sie wirken wie tänzelnde Säulen. Optische Regie führt auf der einen Seite die gekurvte Wand, auf der anderen eine schräggestellte, halbtransparente Wand, die sich überdies in eine Mulde eingräbt. Trotz der schier unendlichen Vielfalt an Materialien behält Soeters die Übersicht: das Ambiente hält Spannung

Quartiers ministériels. Les piliers paraissent ne rien porter mais flotter dans l'espace. D'un côté, le ton est donné par le mur en courbes, de l'autre, par une cloison oblique translucide qui, de plus, s'enfonce dans une fosse dallée. Malgré la variété quasi infinie des matériaux, Soeters garde le contrôle: la tension crée l'équilibre

Biographies | Biographien

Architecture Studio
10, rue Lacuée
75012 Paris, France

Tel: + 33 1 43 45 1800
Fax: + 33 1 43 43 8143

van berkel & bos, architectuur bureau bv
Gebouw De Metropool Weesperstraat 97
1018 VN Amsterdam, The Netherlands

Tel: + 31 20 620 2350
Fax: + 31 20 620 7199

Mario Botta Architetto
Via Ciani 16
6904 Lugano, Switzerland

Tel: + 41 91 9728625
Fax: + 41 91 97 101454

Architecture Studio

Created in 1973, Architecture Studio has six principals: Rodo Tisnado, Martin Robain, Alain Bretagnolle, René-Henri Arnaud, Jean-François Bonne and Laurent-Marc Fischer. Their first major building was the Institut du Monde Arabe (1981–87) designed with Nouvel, Soria and Lezènes. Other significant buildings include the Embassy of France in Muscat, Oman (1987–89); the Lycée du Futur, Jaunay-Clan, France (1986–87); the University Restaurant, Dunkirk, France (1991–93). Current work includes the Institut national du Judo, Paris, France (1988–96); and above all, the European Parliament in Strasbourg, France (1994–97).

Das 1973 gegründete Architecture Studio besteht aus sechs Partnern: Rodo Tisnado, Martin Robain, Alain Bretagnolle, René-Henri Arnaud, Jean-François Bonne und Laurent-Marc Fischer. Das erste bekannte Gebäude der Gruppe war das Institut du Monde Arabe (1981–87), zusammen mit Nouvel, Soria und Lezènes entworfen. Weitere wichtige Bauten sind z.B. die französische Botschaft in Maskat, Oman (1987–89), das Lycée du Futur in Jaunay-Clan, Frankreich (1986–87) und das Universitäts-Restaurant in Dunkerque, Frankreich (1991–93). Zur Zeit beschäftigt sich die Gruppe u.a. mit dem Bau des Institut National du Judo in Paris, Frankreich (1988–96) und vor allem mit dem Europäischen Parlament in Straßburg, Frankreich (1994–97).

Créé en 1973, Architecture Studio compte six associés principaux: Rodo Tisnado, Martin Robain, Alain Bretagnolle, René-Henri Arnaud, Jean-François Bonne et Laurent-Marc Fischer. Leur première œuvre importante a été l'Institut du monde arabe (1981–87), conçu en collaboration avec Nouvel, Soria et Lezènes. Parmi les autres bâtiments importants qu'ils ont construits, on peut citer l'ambassade de France à Muscat (Oman, 1987–89), le Lycée du Futur à Jaunay-Clan (1986–87) et le restaurant universitaire de Dunkerque (1991–93). Actuellement, ils réalisent l'Institut national du judo (Paris, France, 1988–96) et surtout le Parlement européen (Strasbourg, France, 1994–97).

Ben van Berkel

Ben van Berkel was born in Utrecht in 1957 and studied at the Rietveld Academie in Amsterdam and the Architectural Association (AA), London, (AA Honors Diploma, 1987). Worked briefly in the office of Santiago Calatrava, and in 1988, set up practice in Amsterdam with Caroline Bos. Visiting professor at Columbia, New York and visiting critic at Harvard, 1994. Diploma Unit master, AA, London, 1994–95. As well as the Erasmus Bridge in Rotterdam, Van Berkel & Bos Architectural Bureau has built the Karbouw and ACOM (1989–93) office buildings, and the REMU electricity station (1989–93), all in Amersfoort, housing projects and the Aedes East gallery for Kristin Feireiss in Berlin. Current projects include a new museum for Nijmegen and a museum extension in Enschede, Netherlands.

Ben van Berkel wurde 1957 in Utrecht geboren und studierte an der Rietveld Academie in Amsterdam und der Architectural Association (AA) in London (AA Honors Diploma 1987). Er arbeitete kurze Zeit im Büro von Santiago Calatrava und gründete 1988 in Amsterdam zusammen mit Caroline Bos sein eigenes Büro. Gastprofessor an der Columbia University, New York, Gastkritiker in Harvard 1994; Diploma Unit Master an der AA 1994–95. Neben der Erasmusbrug in Rotterdam entwarfen Van Berkel & Bos im niederländischen Amersfoort Bürogebäude für Karbouw und ACOM (1989–93) sowie das REMU-Elektrizitätswerk (1989–93); in Berlin entstanden Wohnbauten und die Aedes East-Galerie für Kristin Feireiss. Zu den aktuellen Projekten zählen ein neues Museum für Nijmegen sowie eine Museumserweiterung in Enschede, Niederlande.

Né à Utrecht en 1957, Ben van Berkel a fait ses études à l'Académie Rietveld d'Amsterdam, puis à Londres, à l'Architectural Association (diplôme avec mention, 1987). Après un bref passage par l'agence de Santiago Calatrava, il ouvre un cabinet avec Caroline Bos en 1988, à Amsterdam. Professeur invité à Columbia University, New York, et critique invité à Harvard, 1994. Directeur de diplôme, AA, Londres, 1994–95. Outre le pont Erasmus déjà cité, le bureau d'architecture Van Berkel & Bos a conçu les bureaux de Karbouw et ACOM (1989–93) ainsi que la centrale électrique REMU (1989–93) à Amersfoort; à Berlin, conception de lotissements et de la galerie Aedes East pour Kristin Feireiss. Parmi les projets en cours: un nouveau musée pour Nijmegen et l'agrandissement du musée de Enschede (Pays-Bas).

Mario Botta

Born in 1943 in Mendrisio, Switzerland, Mario Botta left school at the age of 15 to become an apprentice in a Lugano architectural office. He designed his first house the following year. After completing his studies in Milan and Venice, Botta worked briefly in the entourage of Le Corbusier, Louis Kahn and Luigi Snozzi. He built numerous private houses in Cadenazzo (1970–71), Riva San Vitale (1971–73), or Ligornetto (1975–76). The Médiathèque in Villeurbanne (1984–88) and the Cultural center in Chambéry (1982–87), and the San Francisco Museum of Modern Art, (1990–94) followed. Current projects include the Tamaro Chapel with the artist Enzo Cucchi in Switzerland, a church in Mogno, and a telecommunications center in Bellinzona.

Der 1943 im schweizerischen Mendrisio geborene Mario Botta verließ die Schule bereits mit 15 Jahren, um als Lehrling in einem Architekturbüro in Lugano zu arbeiten. Im darauffolgenden Jahr entwarf er sein erstes Haus. Nach seinem Studium in Mailand und Venedig war er kurzfristig für Le Corbusier, Louis Kahn und Luigi Snozzi tätig. Botta errichtete zahlreiche Privathäuser in Cadenazzo (1970–71), Riva San Vitale (1971–73) und Ligornetto (1975–76), die Médiathèque in Villeurbanne (1984–88), das Kulturzentrum in Chambéry (1982–87) und das San Francisco Museum of Modern Art (1990–94) folgten. Zu seinen aktuellen Bauprojekten zählen die Tamaro-Kapelle in der Schweiz (in Zusammenarbeit mit dem Künstler Enzo Cucchi), eine Kirche in Mogno sowie ein Fernmeldezentrum in Bellinzona.

Né en 1943 à Mendrisio (Suisse), près de la frontière italienne, Mario Botta quitte l'école à l'âge de 15 ans pour devenir apprenti dans un cabinet d'architectes à Lugano. Il conçoit sa première maison l'année suivante. Après avoir poursuivi ses études à Milan puis à Venise, Botta travaille quelque temps dans l'entourage de Le Corbusier, Louis Kahn puis Luigi Snozzi. Il a construit de nombreuses villas à Candenazzo (1970–71), Riva San Vitale (1971–73) et Ligornetto (1975–76). Ont suivi la médiathèque de Villeurbanne (1984–88), le centre culturel de Chambéry (1982–87) et le musée d'art moderne de San Francisco (1990–94). Projets en cours: la chapelle Tamaro, en Suisse (en collaboration avec l'artiste Enzo Cucchi); une église à Mogno, ainsi qu'un centre de télécommunications à Bellinzona.

Erick van Egeraat associated architects bv
Calandstraat 23
3016 CA Rotterdam, The Netherlands

Tel: + 31 10 436 9686
Fax: + 31 10 436 9573

M.F. - France, Massimiliano Fuksas
85 rue du Temple
75003 Paris, France

Tel: + 33 1 44 61 8383
Fax: + 33 1 44 61 8389

Heikkinen-Komonen Architects
Kristianinkatu 11-13
Helsinki 00170, Finland

Tel: + 358 0135 1266
Fax: + 358 0135 1586

Erick van Egeraat

Born in 1956 in Amsterdam, Erick van Egeraat attended the Technical University Delft, Department of Architecture, from which he graduated in 1984. Professional practice since 1981. Co-founder of Mecanoo architects in Delft (1983). Founder of Erick van Egeraat Associated Architects (1995). Recent and current work includes: Faculty building of the Faculties of Physics and Astronomy, University of Leiden (1988–96); Nature and Science Museum, Rotterdam (1989–95); Pop art exhibition, Kunsthal, Rotterdam, 1995; Housing Sternstrasse, Dresden (1994–); Leonardo da Vinci exhibition design, Rotterdam 1995–96, Kunsthal Rotterdam; reconstruction of the "Grote Markt" square east, Groningen; Utrecht Centrum Project, masterplan 1995–96.

Der 1956 in Amsterdam geborene Erick van Egeraat studierte Architektur an der Technischen Hochschule Delft, wo er 1984 sein Examen machte. Seit 1981 ist er praktisch tätig. Mitbegründer der Gruppe Mecanoo in Delft (1983). Gründung von Erick van Egeraat Associated Architects (1995). Zu den aktuellen Projekten zählen: Fakultätsgebäude der Fakultät für Physik und Astronomie der Universität von Leiden (1988–96), Natur- und Wissenschaftsmuseum, Rotterdam (1989–95), Pop art-Ausstellung, Kunsthal Rotterdam (1995), Wohnbauprojekt Sternstraße, Dresden (1994–), Entwurf der Leonardo da Vinci-Ausstellung, Kunsthal Rotterdam (1995–96), Rekonstruktion des »Grote Markt«, Groningen, Bebauungsplan für das Zentrum von Utrecht (1995–96).

Né en 1956 à Amsterdam, Erick van Egeraat a fait ses études à la faculté d'architecture de l'université technique de Delft. Il obtient son diplôme en 1984 et exerce depuis 1981. Co-fondateur de l'agence Mecanoo à Delft (1983). Fondateur de l'agence Erick van Egeraat et Associés (1995). Réalisations récentes et en cours: faculté de physique et d'astronomie de l'université de Leiden (1988–96); Musée de la nature et des sciences (Rotterdam, 1989–95); exposition pop art au Kunsthal de Rotterdam (1995); immeubles d'habitation sur la Sternstrasse, à Dresde (1994–); conception de l'exposition Léonard-de-Vinci au Kunsthal de Rotterdam (1995–96); reconstruction de la place du «Grote Markt» à Groningue; plan d'ensemble du projet Utrecht Centrum (1995–96).

Massimiliano Fuksas

Born in Rome in 1944, Massimiliano Fuksas received his degree from the Faculty of Architecture in Rome in 1969. Created the architectural office "Granma" with Anna Maria Sacconi (1969–88). Having completed a large number of projects in Italy, he began to be known in both Italy and France as of the late 1980s with projects such as his new cemetery in Orvieto (1990), the town hall and library of Cassino (1990) and in France, the Médiathèque, Rézé (1991) and the Ecole nationale d'Ingénieurs de Brest (ENIB, 1992). More recently, he completed the restructuring of a city block on the Rue Candie in Paris (1987–93). Current work includes the Lycée Technique in Alfortville, and the Place des Nations in Geneva, a 150 meter high tower in Vienna and a large shopping center in Salzburg.

Der 1944 in Rom geborene Massimiliano Fuksas erhielt 1969 sein Diplom an der Fakultät für Architektur in Rom. Zusammen mit Anna Maria Sacconi gründete er das Architekturbüro »Granma« (1969–88). Nach einer großen Zahl von Bauten in Italien wurde sein Name gegen Ende der 80er Jahre in Italien und Frankreich mit Projekten wie dem neuen Friedhof von Orvieto (1990), dem Rathaus und der Stadtbücherei von Cassino (1990) bzw. dem Bau der Médiathèque in Rézé (1991) sowie der Ecole nationale d'Ingénieurs de Brest (ENIB, 1992) bekannt. Vor kurzem beendete Fuksas die Wiederbebauung eines Häuserblocks an der Rue Candie in Paris (1987–93). Zu seinen aktuellen Projekten zählen das Lycée Technique in Alfortville, der Place des Nations in Genf, ein 150 Meter hoher Turm in Wien sowie ein großes Einkaufszentrum in Salzburg.

Né en 1944 à Rome, Massimiliano Fuksas obtient son diplôme de la Faculté d'architecture de Rome en 1969. Il crée le cabinet d'architecture «Granma» avec Anna Maria Sacconi (1969–88). Après avoir beaucoup travaillé en Italie, il acquiert une notoriété à la fois en Italie et en France vers la fin des années 1980, grâce à des projets tels que le nouveau cimetière d'Orvieto (1990), l'hôtel de ville et la bibliothèque de Cassino (1990) et, en France, la médiathèque de Rézé (1991) et l'Ecole nationale d'Ingénieurs de Brest (ENIB, 1992). Plus récemment, il a achevé la restructuration d'un immeuble de la rue Candie, à Paris (1987–93). Projets en cours: le lycée technique d'Alfortville; la place des Nations, à Genève; une tour de 150 mètres de haut à Vienne; un grand centre commercial à Salzbourg.

Heikkinen-Komonen

Mikko Heikkinen, b. 1949, Helsinki. M. Arch., Helsinki University of Technology, 1975. Created Heikkinen-Komonen Architects in 1974. Teacher at Helsinki University of Technology, 1977, 1978, 1987, 1989. Visiting Critic at University College of Dublin, University of Virginia, Städelschule Frankfurt and Virginia Tech. Markku Komonen, b. 1945, Helsinki. M. Arch., Helsinki University of Technology, 1974. Editor-in-chief of Arkkitehti Magazine, 1977–80. Director, Exhibition Department, Museum of Finnish Architecture 1978–86. Professor at Helsinki University of Technology since 1992. Recent work includes: Heureka Finnish Science Center, Helsinki, 1988; Royal Theater, Copenhagen (competition) 1995; McDonald's Headquarters, Helsinki, 1995–; European Film College, Ebeltoft, Denmark, 1990–92; Passenger Terminal, Rovaniemi Airport, 1989–92.

Mikko Heikkinen: geb. 1949 in Helsinki. 1975 M. Arch., Techn. Univer. Helsinki. Gründung von Heikkinen-Komonen Architects 1974. Dozent an der Techn. Univer. Helsinki 1977, 1978, 1987, 1989. Gastkritiker an mehreren Hochschulen. Markku Komonen, geb. 1945 in Helsinki. 1974 M. Arch., Techn. Univer. Helsinki. 1977–1980 Chefredakteur des Magazins »Arkkitehti«. Direktor der Ausstellungsabteilung am Museum für Finnische Architektur 1978–86. Seit 1992 Professor an der Techn. Univer. Helsinki. Aktuelle Bauten: Heureka Finnisches Wissenschaftszentrum, Helsinki (1988), Royal Theater, Kopenhagen (Wettbewerb 1995), McDonald's Headquarters, Helsinki (1995–), European Film College, Ebeltoft, Dänemark (1990–92), Passagierterminal, Rovaniemi Airport (1989–92).

Mikko Heikkinen, né en 1949 à Helsinki. Obtient une M. Arch. à l'université technologique d'Helsinki en 1975. Crée le cabinet Heikkinen-Komonen en 1974. Enseigne à l'université technologique d'Helsinki en 1977, 1978, 1987 et 1989. Critique invité de: University College of Dublin, University of Virginia, Städelschule Frankfurt et Virginia Tech. Markku Komonen, né en 1945 à Helsinki. Obtient une M. Arch. à l'université technologique d'Helsinki en 1974. Rédacteur en chef de la revue «Arkkitehti» de 1977 à 1980. Responsable des expositions au Musée de l'architecture finlandaise de 1978 à 1986. Professeur à l'université technologique d'Helsinki depuis 1992. Récentes réalisations: Heureka, le Centre finlandais des sciences (Helsinki, 1988); Théâtre Royal-Nouveau Théâtre, Copenhague (concours limité, 1995); siège social de McDonald's (Helsinki, 1995–); Ecole européenne du cinéma (Ebeltoft, Danemark, 1990–92); terminal de l'aéroport de Rovaniemi, 1989–92.

Juha Leiviskä
Ratakatu 14A12
00120 Helsinki, Finland

Tel: + 358 0 630 722
Fax: + 358 0 630 726

Dominique Perrault, Architecte
26/34 rue Bruneseau
75013, Paris, France

Tel: + 33 1 44 06 0000
Fax: + 33 1 44 06 0099

Richard Rogers Partnership
Thames Wharf, Rainville Road
London W6 9HA, England

Tel: + 44 171 385 1235
Fax: + 44 171 385 8409

Juha Leiviskä

Born in 1936 in Helsinki, Juha Leiviskä graduated from the Helsinki University of Technology in 1963, and after initially collaborating with Bertel Saarnio on Kouvola Town Hall has been in practice on his own since 1967, in partnership with Vilhelm Helander since 1978.
St. Thomas's Church, Oslo (1970–75) was his first major project. He has entered over 40 competitions, such as those for the Helsinki Museum of Modern Art (1993), or the Reichstag (1992) and built 18 buildings of various kinds including private residences, housing, libraries, schools, day care centers, the Embassy of the Federal Republic of Germany in Helsinki (1986–93) and a considerable number of churches and parish centers. Winner, 1995 Carlsberg Prize.

Der 1936 in Helsinki geborene Juha Leiviskä schloß 1963 sein Studium an der Technischen Universität Helsinki ab. Nach kurzer Zusammenarbeit mit Bertel Saarnio (Entwurf des Rathauses von Kouvola) gründete er 1967 sein eigenes Büro und arbeitet seit 1978 in Partnerschaft mit Vilhelm Helander. Leiviskäs erstes großes Projekt war die St. Thomas-Kirche in Oslo (1970–75). Er beteiligte sich an über 40 Architekturwettbewerben, u.a. für das Helsinki Museum of Modern Art (1993) und den Reichstag (1992) und erbaute 18 Gebäude verschiedenster Art – Privathäuser, Wohnbauten, Büchereien, Schulen und Tagesstätten – sowie die Botschaft der Bundesrepublik Deutschland in Helsinki (1986–93) und eine große Zahl von Kirchen und Gemeindezentren. Gewinner des Carlsberg-Preises 1995.

Né à Helsinki en 1936, Juha Leiviskä est diplômé de l'université technologique d'Helsinki (1963). Après avoir collaboré à la conception de l'hôtel de ville de Kouvola réalisé par Bertel Saarnio, il s'installe à son compte en 1967. Depuis 1978, il est associé avec Vilhelm Helander. Son premier projet important a été l'église Saint-Thomas à Oslo (1970–75). Il a participé a plus de 40 concours, parmi lesquels ceux organisés pour le musée d'art moderne d'Helsinki (1993) et pour le Reichstag (1992). Il a construit 18 bâtiments de types divers: maisons individuelles, ensembles de logements, bibliothèques, écoles, crèches, un nombre considérable d'églises et de centres paroissiaux, ainsi que l'ambassade d'Allemagne à Helsinki (1986-93). Lauréat du prix Carlsberg 1995.

Dominique Perrault

Dominique Perrault was born in 1953 in Clermont-Ferrand, France. He received his diploma as an architect from the Beaux-Arts UP 6 in Paris in 1978. He received a further degree in urbanism at the Ecole nationale des Ponts et Chaussées, Paris in 1979. He created his own firm in 1981 in Paris. Built work includes the Engineering School (ESIEE) in Marne-la-Vallée (1984–87); the Hôtel industriel Jean-Baptiste Berlier, Paris (1986–90); and the Hôtel du département de la Meuse, Bar-le-Duc, France (1988–94). Current work includes the Olympic Velodrome, swimming and diving pool, Berlin, Germany (1992–98); and a large-scale study of the urbanism of Bordeaux (1992–2000).

Dominique Perrault wurde 1953 in Clermont-Ferrand geboren. Er erhielt 1978 sein Diplom als Architekt an der Beaux-Arts UP 6 sowie 1979 einen Abschluß in Urbanistik an der Ecole nationale des Ponts et Chaussées in Paris. 1981 Gründung einer eigenen Firma in Paris. Zu den fertiggestellten Bauten gehören die Ingenieurschule (ESIEE) in Marne-la-Vallée (1984–87), das Hôtel industriel Jean-Baptiste Berlier, Paris (1986–90) sowie das Hôtel du département de la Meuse, Bar-le-Duc (1988–94). Gegenwärtig arbeitet Perrault am Olympischen Velodrom und einer Schwimmhalle in Berlin (1992–98) sowie an einer großangelegten stadtplanerischen Studie von Bordeaux (1992–2000).

Dominique Perrault est né en 1953 à Clermont-Ferrand. Il obtient son diplôme d'architecture aux Beaux-Arts de Paris (UP 6) en 1978, et un diplôme d'urbanisme à l'Ecole nationale des ponts et chaussées en 1979. Il crée son propre cabinet en 1981 à Paris. Il a réalisé l'ESIEE, école d'ingénieurs située à Marne-la-Vallée (1984–87); l'hôtel industriel Jean-Baptiste Berlier, à Paris (1986–90); l'hôtel du département de la Meuse, à Bar-le-Duc (1988–94). Projets en cours: un vélodrome et une piscine olympiques à Berlin (1992–98); une étude d'urbanisme à grande échelle pour la ville de Bordeaux (1992–2000).

Richard Rogers

Born in Florence, Italy, of British parents in 1933, Richard Rogers studied at the Architectural Association in London (1954–59). He received his M. Arch. degree from the Yale University School of Architecture in 1962. Created partnerships with his wife Su Rogers, Norman and Wendy Foster (Team 4, London, 1964–66); and with Renzo Piano in London, Paris and Genoa (1971–77). He created Richard Rogers Partnership in London (1977). He has taught at Yale, and been Chairman of the Trustees of the Tate Gallery, London (1981–89). Main buildings include: the Centre Georges Pompidou, Paris (with Renzo Piano, 1971–77); Lloyd's of London, headquarters (1978–86); Channel 4 television headquarters, London (1990–94); Daimler Benz office building, Potsdamer Platz, Berlin (1994); Bordeaux Palais de Justice (1993–).

Richard Rogers wurde 1933 in Florenz als Sohn englischer Eltern geboren und studierte an der Architectural Association in London (1954–59). 1962 erwarb er den Master of Architecture an der Yale University School of Architecture. Rogers arbeitete in Partnerschaft mit seiner Frau Su Rogers, Norman und Wendy Foster (Team 4, London 1964–66) sowie zusammen mit Renzo Piano in London, Paris und Genua (1971–77). 1977 Gründung von Richard Rogers Partnership in London. Rogers unterrichtete in Yale und war Vorsitzender des Kuratoriums der Tate Gallery, London (1981–89). Zu seinen wichtigsten Bauten zählen: Centre Georges Pompidou, Paris (mit Renzo Piano, 1971–77), Lloyd's of London, Headquarters (1978–86), Channel 4 Television Headquarters, London (1990–94), Daimler-Benz Bürogebäude, Potsdamer Platz, Berlin (1994), Bordeaux Palais de Justice (1993–).

Né à Florence (Italie) de parents britanniques en 1933, Richard Rogers a fait ses études à l'Architectural Association de Londres (1954–59). Il obtient son diplôme à la Yale University School of Architecture en 1962. S'associe avec son épouse Su Rogers et avec Norman et Wendy Foster (Team 4, Londres, 1964–66); puis avec Renzo Piano à Londres, Paris et Gênes (1971–77). Création de Richard Rogers Partnership à Londres en 1977. A enseigné à Yale; président du conseil d'administration de la Tate Gallery de 1981 à 1989. Principales réalisations: Centre Pompidou, Paris (en collaboration avec Renzo Piano, 1971–77); siège social de la Lloyd's of London (1978–86); siège social de la chaîne Channel 4, Londres (1990–94); immeuble de bureaux pour Daimler Benz, Potsdamer Platz, Berlin (1994); palais de justice de Bordeaux (1993–).

Aldo Rossi Studio di Architettura
Via Santa Maria alla Porta, 9
20123 Milan, Italy

Tel: + 39 2 7201 0046
Fax: + 39 2 8901 0633

Schneider + Schumacher
Schleusenstr. 17
60327 Frankfurt, Germany

Tel: + 49 69 23 75 75
Fax: + 49 69 23 75 99

Architekten Schweger + Partner
Poststraße 12
20354 Hamburg, Germany

Tel: + 49 40 35 09 590
Fax: + 49 40 35 12 20

Aldo Rossi

Aldo Rossi, b. 1931, Milan. Studied at Milan Polytechnic, 1949–59. Began working with Ernesto Rogers on *Casabella-Continuità* in 1956 and became editor in 1964. His 1966 book *Architecture and the City* is considered a significant study of urban design and thinking. 1965, appointed professor at Milan Polytechnic, professor at Federal Polytechnic of Zurich (ETH), 1972; University of Venice, 1973. 1990 Pritzker Prize. Significant work includes: Cemetery of San Cataldo, Modena, Italy (1971–90); Teatro del Mondo, Venice, Italy, Venice Biennale (1980); Südliche Friedrichstadt Housing Complex, Berlin, Germany (1981–88); Centro Torri Commercial Center, Parma, Italy (1985–88); Il Palazzo Hotel, Fukuoka, Japan (1989); Vassiviere Modern Art Museum, Clermont-Ferrand, France (1988–90); Celebration Place, Celebration, Florida (1991–95); Office Tower, Mexico City, Mexico (1994–) in progress.

Aldo Rossi (geb. 1931 in Mailand). 1949–59 Studium am Mailänder Polytechnikum. Ab 1956 Zusammenarbeit mit Ernesto Rogers für »Casabella-Continuità« und ab 1964 Herausgeber. 1966 erschien sein Buch »L'Architettura della Città«; gilt als bedeutende Studie städtischen Planens und Denkens. Seit 1965 Professor am Mailänder Polytechnikum; 1972 Professor an der Eidgenössischen Techn. Hochschule in Zürich (ETH) und 1973 an der Universität Venedig. Pritzker Preis 1990. Wichtige Arbeiten: Friedhof von San Cataldo, Modena, Italien (1971–90), Teatro del Mondo, Biennale Venedig, Italien (1980), Wohnkomplex Südliche Friedrichstadt, Berlin (1981–88), Centro Torri, Parma, Italien (1985–88), Il Palazzo Hotel, Fukuoka, Japan (1989), Vassiviere Modern Art Museum, Clermont-Ferrand, Frankreich (1988–90), Celebration Place, Celebration, Florida (1991–95), Office Tower, Mexico City, Mexiko (1994–).

Aldo Rossi, né en 1931 à Milan. Etudes à l'Institut polytechnique de Milan (1949–59). Commence à travailler avec Ernesto Rogers pour «Casabella-Continuità» en 1956; rédacteur en chef en 1964. Il publie en 1966 «L'Architecture et la Ville», considéré comme une étude importante dans le domaine de la conception et de la réflexion urbanistique. En 1965, il est nommé professeur à l'Institut polytechnique de Milan. Enseigne à l'Institut polytechnique fédéral de Zurich (ETH) en 1972 et à l'université de Venise en 1973. Obtient le prix Pritzker en 1990. Principales réalisations: cimetière de San Cataldo, Modène (1971–90); Teatro del Mondo, Venise, Biennale de Venise (1980); ensemble d'habitations Südliche Friedrichstadt, Berlin (1981–88); centre commercial Centro Torri, Parme (1985–88); Il Palazzo Hotel, Fukuoka, Japon (1989); musée d'Art moderne Vassivière, Clermont-Ferrand, France (1988–90); Celebration Place, Celebration, Floride (1991–95); Office Tower, Mexico (1994–) en cours de réalisation.

Schneider + Schumacher

Till Schneider, b. 1959, studied at University of Kaiserslautern, diploma from the Technische Hochschule, Darmstadt. Postgraduate studies at the Staatliche Hochschule für Bildende Künste, Städelschule, Frankfurt, in the class of Peter Cook. Worked in the offices of Eisele + Fritz, Darmstadt, and Robert Mürb, Karlsruhe. Created his own office in Frankfurt with Michael Schumacher (1988). Michael Schumacher, b. 1957, also studied at the University of Kaiserslautern. Postgraduate studies at the Staatliche Hochschule für Bildende Künste, Städelschule, Frankfurt, in the class of Peter Cook. Worked in the office of Norman Foster, London, and Braun & Schlockermann, Frankfurt before 1988. Most important built work: office building for J. Walter Thompson, Frankfurt, (1994–95). Most important current job: administrative building for KPMG (Deutsche Treuhandgesellschaft), Leipzig, mid-1997 completion.

Till Schneider, geb. 1959, studierte an der Uni Kaiserslautern. Diplom an der Techn. Hochschule Darmstadt. Postgraduiertenstudium an der Staatl. Hochschule für Bildende Künste, Städelschule, Frankfurt, Klasse von Peter Cook. Arbeitete für Eisele + Fritz in Darmstadt und Robert Mürb, Karlsruhe. 1988 Gründung eines Büros in Frankfurt, zusammen mit Michael Schumacher. Michael Schumacher, 1957 geb., studierte an der Uni Kaiserslautern. Postgraduiertenstudium an der Staatl. Hochschule für Bildende Künste, Städelschule, Frankfurt, Klasse von Peter Cook. Bis 1988 arbeitete er für die Büros von Norman Foster, London und Braun & Schlockermann, Frankfurt. Bedeutendstes Bauwerk: Bürogebäude für J. Walter Thompson, Frankfurt (1994–95). Wichtigster derzeitiger Bauauftrag: Verwaltungsgebäude der KPMG (Deutsche Treuhandgesellschaft), Leipzig; gepl. Fertigstellung Mitte 1997.

Né en 1959, Till Schneider est diplômé de l'université de Kaiserslautern et de la Technische Hochschule de Darmstadt. Troisième cycle à la Staatl. Hochschule für Bildende Künste, Städelschule, à Francfort, dans la promotion de Peter Cook. A travaillé pour Eisele + Fritz, à Darmstadt, et pour Robert Mürb, à Karlsruhe. Ouvre sa propre agence à Francfort avec Michael Schumacher en 1988. Né en 1957, Michael Schumacher est diplômé de l'université de Kaiserslautern. Troisième cycle à la Staatliche Hochschule für Bildende Künste, Städelschule, à Francfort, dans la promotion de Peter Cook. Avant 1988, travaille pour Norman Foster, à Londres, et pour Braun & Schlockermann, à Francfort. Principale réalisation: immeuble de bureaux pour J. Walter Thompson, à Francfort (1994–95). Principal projet en cours: bâtiment administratif pour KPMG (Deusche Treuhandgesellschaft) à Leipzig; livraison vers la fin du premier semestre 1997.

Schweger + Partner

Born in 1935 in Medias, Rumania, Peter Schweger attended the Technical University, Budapest, and the University of Zurich, Eidgenössische Technische Hochschule Zurich (ETH), 1959 diploma. From 1959 to 1962 he had an office in Vienna. Visiting professorship at school of arts, Hochschule für Bildende Künste, Hamburg and visiting professorship at the Technical University of Hannover's Institute for Design and Architecture (1968–69). Founded office of Graaf + Schweger in 1968 (1987 Architekten Schweger + Partner: P. Schweger, F. Wöhler, H. Reifenstein, B. Kohl and W. Schneider). Professor at the Technical University of Hannover, Institute for Design and Architecture, Technische Universität Hannover (1972). Current work includes: Poseidon-Haus, Hamburg (office building) (1990–95); Deutscher Industrie- und Handelstag (headquarters), Berlin (1994–97); and The Center for Art and Media Technology, Karlsruhe (1993–97).

Der 1935 im rumänischen Medias geborene Peter Schweger besuchte die Techn. Hochschule Budapest und die Eidgenössische Techn. Hochschule (ETH) in Zürich. Von 1959 bis 1962 Büro in Wien. Gastprofessur an der Hochschule für Bildende Künste Hamburg sowie am Institut für Architektur und Design der Technischen Hochschule Hannover (1968–69). 1968 Gründung des Büros Graaf + Schweger (1987 Architekten Schweger + Partner: P. Schweger, F. Wöhler, H. Reifenstein, B. Kohl und W. Schneider). 1972 Professor an der Technischen Hochschule Hannover, Institut für Architektur und Design. Laufende Projekte: Poseidon-Haus, Hamburg (Bürogebäude) (1990–95); Deutscher Industrie- und Handelstag (Zentrale), Berlin (1994–97); Zentrum für Kunst- und Medientechnologie, Karlsruhe (1993–97).

Né en 1935 à Medias (Roumanie), Peter Schweger a fait ses études à l'université technique de Budapest et à l'université de Zurich (diplômé de la Eidgenössische Technische Hochschule de Zurich en 1959). De 1959 à 1962, il exerce dans sa propre agence à Vienne. Professeur invité à la faculté des arts de la Hochschule für Bildende Künste, à Hambourg. Professeur invité à la faculté technique de l'Institut de design et d'architecture de Hanovre (1968–69). Crée l'agence Graaf + Schweger en 1968 puis, en 1987, Architekten Schweger + Partner: P. Schweger, F. Wöhler, H. Reifenstein, B. Kohl et W. Schneider). Professeur à l'Institut de design et d'architecture de l'université technique de Hanovre (1972). Réalisations récentes ou en cours: Poseidon-Haus (Hambourg, 1990–95), siège social du Deutscher Industrie- und Handelstag (Berlin 1994–97), Centre d'art et de technologie des médias (Karlsruhe, 1993–97).

Alvaro Siza Arquitecto, Lda
Rua da Alegria 399, A-2°
4000 Porto, Portugal

Tel: + 351 257 0850
Fax: + 351 251 03518

Valode & Pistre et associés
23, rue du Renard
75004 Paris, France

Tel: + 33 1 42 78 4895
Fax: + 33 1 42 78 5181

Alvaro Siza

Born in Matosinhos, Portugal, in 1933, Alvaro Siza studied at the University of Porto School of Architecture (1949–55). He created his own practice in 1954, and worked with Fernando Tavora from 1955 to 1958. He has been a Professor of Construction at the University of Porto since 1976. He received the European Community's Mies van der Rohe Prize in 1988 and the Pritzker Prize in 1992. He built a large number of small-scale projects in Portugal, and more recently, he has worked on the restructuring of the Chiado, Lisbon, Portugal (1989–); the Meteorology Center, Barcelona, Spain (1989–92); the Vitra Furniture Factory, Weil am Rhein, Germany (1991–94); the Oporto School of Architecture, Oporto University (1986–95); and the University of Aveiro Library, Aveiro, Portugal (1988–95).

Alvaro Siza wurde 1933 in Matosinhos, Portugal, geboren und studierte an der Schule für Architektur der Universität Porto (1949–55). Siza gründete 1954 sein eigenes Büro und arbeitete von 1955 bis 1958 mit Fernando Tavora zusammen. Seit 1976 Professor für Bautechnik an der Universität Porto. Siza erhielt 1988 den Mies van der Rohe-Preis der Europäischen Gemeinschaft und 1992 den Pritzker Preis. Er erstellte eine große Zahl kleiner Bauprojekte in Portugal. Zu den Projekten der letzten Jahre gehören: Wiederaufbau des Lissaboner Einkaufsviertels Chiado, Portugal (1989–), Meteorologisches Zentrum, Barcelona, Spanien (1989–92), Möbelfabrik Vitra, Weil am Rhein (1991–94), Schule für Architektur, Universität Porto (1986–95), Bibliothek der Universität Aveiro, Portugal (1988–95).

Né à Matosinhos (Portugal) en 1933, Alvaro Siza a fait ses études à la faculté d'architecture de l'université de Porto (1949–55). Il ouvre son cabinet en 1954 et travaille avec Fernando Tavora de 1955 à 1958. Enseigne les techniques de construction à l'université de Porto depuis 1976. Obtient le prix Mies van der Rohe de la Communauté européenne en 1988 et le prix Pritzker en 1992. Siza a réalisé de nombreux projets de taille modeste au Portugal, et, plus récemment, il a travaillé sur les projets suivants: restructuration du Chiado, à Lisbonne, Portugal (1989–); Centre météorologique de Barcelone (1989–92); usine de meubles Vitra, Weil am Rhein (1991–94); école d'architecture de Porto (1986–95); bibliothèque de l'université de Aveiro (Portugal, 1988–95).

Valode & Pistre

Denis Valode was born in 1946, and was a Professor of architecture at the Ecole des Beaux Arts (UP1 and UP2) from 1972 to 1985. Jean Pistre was born in 1951. They first worked together in 1977 and established their office Valode & Pistre in 1980. Built work includes the renovation of the CAPC, Bordeaux (1990) and the installation of the Direction régionale des Affaires Culturelles (Regional Cultural Authority) in an 18th century building, Lyon (1987–92); CFDT Headquarters, Paris (1986–90); Shell Headquarters, Reuil-Malmaison, France (1988–91); EPS Schlumberger, Clamart (1989–93); Leonardo da Vinci University, Courbevoie, France (1992–95); Air France Headquarters, Roissy Airport (1992–95). Outside of France, they have worked on a planned Media Tower, Babelsberg, Potsdam (1993), and offices and a hotel also for Potsdam (1993).

Denis Valode wurde 1946 geboren und unterrichtete von 1972 bis 1985 als Professor für Architektur an der Ecole des Beaux Arts (UP1 und UP2). Jean Pistre wurde 1951 geboren. Beide arbeiteten 1977 erstmals zusammen und gründeten 1980 das Büro Valode & Pistre. Zu ihren Arbeiten zählen die Neugestaltung des CAPC, Bordeaux (1990), die Einrichtung der Lyoner Direction régionale des Affaires Culturelles in einem Gebäude aus dem 18. Jahrhundert (1987–92), CFDT Zentrale, Paris (1986–90), Shell Headquarters, Reuil-Malmaison, Frankreich (1988–91), EPS Schlumberger, Clamart (1989–93), Leonardo da Vinci-Universität, Courbevoie, Frankreich (1992–95), Air France Zentrale, Flughafen Roissy (1992–95). Außerhalb Frankreichs arbeiteten Valode & Pistre an der Planung eines Media-Turms in Babelsberg (1993) sowie an Bürogebäuden und einem Hotel in Potsdam (1993).

Denis Valode est né en 1946. Il enseigne l'architecture aux Beaux-Arts (UP1 et UP2) de 1972 à 1985. Jean Pistre est né en 1951. Ils commencent à travailler ensemble en 1977 et ouvrent l'agence Valode & Pistre en 1980. Réalisations: rénovation du CAPC à Bordeaux (1990) et installation de la Direction régionale des affaires culturelles dans un immeuble du XVIIIe siècle à Lyon (1987–92); siège de la CFDT à Paris (1986–90); siège social de Shell à Rueil-Malmaison (1988–91); EPS Schlumberger à Clamart (1989–93); université Léonard-de-Vinci à Courbevoie (1992–95); immeuble d'Air France à l'aéroport de Roissy (1992–95). A l'extérieur de la France, ils ont travaillé sur le projet d'une Tour des médias à Babelsberg, Potsdam (1993), ainsi que sur des bureaux et un hôtel également à Potsdam (1993).

Index

Credits | Fotonachweis | Crédits photographiques

l. = left | links | à gauche
r. = right | rechts | à droite
t. = top | oben | ci-dessus
c. = centre | Mitte | centre
b. = bottom | unten | ci-dessous

2	© Photo: Christian Richters
6	© Photo: Jeff Goldberg	Esto
9	© Aldo Rossi
10	© Photo: Christian Richters
13	© Photo: Bernadette Grimmenstein
14	© Photo: Jeff Goldberg	Esto
17	© Photo: Hayes Davidson	Richard Davies
18	© Photo: Hayes Davidson
21	22	© Christo	Photo: Wolfgang Volz
25	© Yadegar Asisi
26	© Photo: Jeff Goldberg	Esto
29	© Photo: Arno de la Chapelle
30	© Photo: Jeff Goldberg	Esto
33 t.	© Photo: Ben van Berkel
33 b.	© Ben van Berkel
34	© Photo: Hélène Binet
37	38	© Photo: Christian Richters
41	© Photo: Archipress	Stéphane Couturier
42	© Photo: Archipress	Alain Goustard
42	43 t.	© Valode & Pistre
45	© Photo: Arnaud Carpentier
46	49	© Photo: Christian Richters
50	53	© Photo: Paul Raftery	Arcaid
54	© Aki Furudate
56	© Photo: Antonio Martinelli
57	© M. Fuksas
59	© Photo: Hisao Suzuki	Archivo Eye
60–61	© Photo: Richard Bryant	Vitra
62	© Photo: Archipress	Stéphane Couturier
63	© Photo: Thibaud de St. Chamas
64–66	© Photo: Archipress	Stéphane Couturier
67 l.	© Photo: Michel Moch
67 r.	© Photo: Urquijo Rhiel
68	© Photo: Jan Derwig
69	© Photo: Hans-Jürgen Commerell
70	© Photo: Jan Derwig
71	72 b.	© Ben van Berkel
72	73 t.	© Photo: Jan Derwig
73	© Photo: Jan Derwig
74	© Ben van Berkel
75 t.	© Photo: Hans-Jürgen Commerell
75 b.	© Photo: Jan Derwig
76	© Photo: Arnaud Carpentier
77	© Photo: Marcel Imsand
78	© Mario Botta
79–81	© Photo: Arnaud Carpentier
82 t.	© Mario Botta
82 b.	© Photo: Arnaud Carpentier
83 l.	© Photo: Arnaud Carpentier
83 r.	© Mario Botta
84	© Photo: Christian Richters
85	© Photo: Vincent Mentzel

86 t.	© Photo: Christian Richters
86 b.	© Erick van Egeraat
87 t.	© Photo: Christian Richters
87 b.l.	© Erick van Egeraat
87 b.r.	© Photo: Christian Richters
88	89 t.	© Photo: Christian Richters
89 b.	© Erick van Egeraat
90–91	© Photo: Christian Richters
92 t.r.	© Photo: Christian Richters
92 b.r.	© Erick van Egeraat
92 t.l.	© Erick van Egeraat
92 b.l.	© Photo: Christian Richters
93	© Photo: Christian Richters
94	© M. Fuksas
95	© Photo: Roger Guillemot
96	© M. Fuksas
97	© Photo: Aki Furudate
98	© Photo: Antonio Martinelli
100 t.	© Photo: Antonio Martinelli
100 c.	© M. Fuksas
100 b.	© Photo: Antonio Martinelli
101	© Photo: Antonio Martinelli
102	© Photo: Jeff Goldberg	Esto
103 l.	© Photo: Perrti Nisonen
103 r.	© Photo: Heikkinen-Komonen
104–106	© Photo: Jeff Goldberg	Esto
107 t.l.	© Heikkinen-Komonen
107 t.r.	© Photo: Jeff Goldberg	Esto
107 c.	© Photo: Jeff Goldberg	Esto
107 b.	© Heikkinen-Komonen
108	© Photo: Arno de la Chapelle
109	© Photo: Sakari Viika
110	111 b.	© Juha Leiviskä
111 t.	r. 112–113	© Photo: Arno de la Chapelle
114	© Photo: Christian Richters
115	© Photo: Cira Moro
116	© Photo: Christian Richters
117–119	© Photo: Christian Richters
119 r.	© Dominique Perrault
120	121	© Photo: Archipress	Michel Denancé
122	123	© Photo: Christian Richters
124	© Photo: Paul Raftery	Arcaid
125	© Photo: Seiji Okumiya
126	© Richard Rogers
127	© Photo: Paul Raftery	Arcaid
128	129	© Photo: Paul Raftery	Arcaid
129 t.	© Richard Rogers
129 c.	© Photo: Paul Raftery	Arcaid
129 b.	© Richard Rogers
130	© Photo: Christian Richters
131	© Photo: Luca Vignelli

133 t.	© Photo: Christian Richters
133 b.	© Etienne van Sloun
134–135	© Photo: Christian Richters
135 t.	© Photo: Christian Richters
135 b.	© Aldo Rossi
136–138	© Photo: Christian Richters
139 r.	© Photo: Christian Richters
139 l.	© Photo: Etienne van Sloun	Ramaekers
140	© Photo: F. Busam	Architekturphoto
141	© Photo: Schneider & Schumacher
142	© Photo: Jörg Hempel	Architekton
143 t.	© Photo: Jörg Hempel	Architekton
143 b.	© Photo: Schneider & Schumacher
144	© Photo: Jörg Hempel	Architekton
145 t.	© Photo: F. Busam	Architekturphoto
145 c.	© Schneider & Schumacher
145 b.	© Photo: Jörg Hempel	Architekton
146	© Photo: Bernadette Grimmenstein
147	© Photo: Tom Höfermann
148	© Schweger + Partner
149	© Photo: Wolfgang Neeb
150–152	© Photo: Bernadette Grimmenstein
153 t.	© Schweger + Partner
153 b.	© Photo: Wolfgang Neeb	Kunst: Panamarenko
154	© Photo: Bernhard Kroll
154	155	© Photo: Wolfgang Neeb
156	© Photo: Jeff Goldberg	Esto
157	© Photo: Tereza Siza
158–160	© Photo: Jeff Goldberg	Esto
161 t.	c.	© Photo: Jeff Goldberg	Esto
161 b.	© Alvaro Siza
162	© Photo: Archipress	Alain Goustard
163	© Photo: Valode & Pistre
164	© Valode & Pistre
165 t.	© Photo: Archipress	Alain Goustard
165 b.	© Photo: Valode & Pistre
166	© Photo: Archipress	Alain Goustard
167 l.	© Photo: Valode & Pistre
167 r.	© Photo: Archipress	Alain Goustard
168–169	© Photo: Archipress	Alain Goustard

The publisher and editor wish to thank each of the architects and photographers for their kind assistance.